# WHAT PEOPLE ARE SAYING
## ABOUT *CHANGING LONDON*

'London is a great city but it could be even better. We need to make it more affordable, fight inequality and stand up for the diversity which makes London a great city. This book has interesting ideas on all of this.' — **Diane Abbott**

'London has it all, but underneath the surface our city faces an inequality crisis. We are becoming a city of the rich and the rest, living together but growing apart. We are building more luxury flats than ever but fewer than half the homes we need; we are home to more millionaires and billionaires than anywhere else in Europe yet more than 70,000 children have no home at all; and we are officially the number one city for opportunity on the planet yet hundreds of thousands of our young people can't find a job. The next mayor of London has to address the inequality pulling our city apart, there's no question about that. This book helps show the way.' — **Tessa Jowell**

'*Changing London* has shown how politics should be done. David and the team have produced a wide range of bold and radical ideas for making London a city that actually works for Londoners. The focus on tackling inequality and building stronger, fairer communities is exactly what our city needs. Most importantly, they have done it through collaboration with real Londoners. Working with ordinary people to hear about how they live their lives, the problems they face day-to-day and what help they need to build a better future for themselves and their families. This is a hugely exciting project.' — **Sadiq Khan**

'*Changing London* has led the way in producing serious, sensible and innovative ideas for the type of London we all want to see. It is this kind of fresh thinking that is required if we are to build a city of opportunity for all Londoners; tackling the housing crisis, keeping transport affordable and creating new skilled jobs for Londoners will not happen without ambitious ideas and a political commitment to implementing them. But nor will it happen without the input and support of Londoners – that's why *Changing London*'s focus on involving people across our city is so important. I recommend this book to anyone with an interest in London's future.' — **David Lammy**

'This is an amazing publication. Not just because the ideas fill me with the hope that London can become a home for our shared humanity but also because it was created out of a caring, collaborative, inquiring and imaginative spirit – which are exactly the traits we need for London to become the city of our dreams. Please read it, share it, critique it, build it and make it happen.' — **Neal Lawson**, Chair, Compass

'For Londoners, and for all those who care about its future, the mayor plays a decisive role in shaping the kind of capital we live in and love. This new book collects together the ideas and experiences of people who care about London's diverse and disadvantaged communities without whose help the city simply would not function. David Robinson became an East London community worker before he left school and has stuck at it ever since. No one has more experience and insight than David into the huge challenges and opportunities of London. This book will open eyes for all those struggling with the complexities and contradictions of London's government.' — **Anne Power**, Professor of Social Policy, LSE

'Politics in modern society is more than casting a vote. The electorate have a voice, views and experience of life in Britain's capital city that have little room to germinate let alone be heard and discussed in the tra-ditional format of the hustings. *Changing London* breaks that mould. For eighteen months, Londoners, in all their diversity, have contributed in a collaborative, radical process, via the internet, to offer fresh ideas and a robust different vision of how London ought to be – and can be. Every mayoral candidate should take heed. This is the new politics.' — **Yvonne Roberts**, Chief Leader writer, *The Observer*

'I greatly applaud *Changing London*'s efforts to widen interest in the may-oralty and the role of the mayor. It is a great institution but it is relatively new and many people do not understand the importance of the mayor in determining priorities for our great city. I particularly like the sug-gestions to engage local communities and people in discussions about the mayor, as sometimes City Hall can appear remote from ordinary Londoners.' — **Christian Wolmar**

'I don't think I've ever read anything which so powerfully, and practi-cally, makes the case for community-led local solutions to big problems. It's something to return to time and again as a source of ideas and in-spiration. And it's beautifully written.' — **Steve Wyler**, former Chief Executive of Locality

# CHANGING LONDON

# CHANGING LONDON
## A ROUGH GUIDE FOR THE NEXT LONDON MAYOR

## DAVID ROBINSON
## WILL HORWITZ

LONDON PUBLISHING PARTNERSHIP

Published by London Publishing Partnership
www.londonpublishingpartnership.co.uk

ISBN: 978-1-907994-47-0 (pbk)

A catalogue record for this book is
available from the British Library

Copy-edited and typeset by
T&T Productions Ltd, London
www.tandtproductions.com

Cover cartoon drawn by Kipper Williams
Front cover layout by Alex Pickup

The font used for the quotes on the front and back covers
is called Clarendon. It is a traditional slab serif created by
Robert Besley in London in the 1800s. A printer and civic
activist, he went on to become Sheriff of the City of London
in 1863 and the Lord Mayor of London in 1869.

Printed by Page Bros, Norwich

# CONTENTS

# FOREWORD

This is a book about politics but it is also, for me, a book about London, the greatest city in the world and the most beautiful. It's a city in which to walk and discover the hidden backstreets, the squares and small parks.

Start around Brick Lane and walk westwards into the global financial powerhouse of the City of London. Walk to Aldgate and down to Cornhill, past Bank and Mansion House and down to Blackfriars and the Embankment to see the Thames in full flow. Walk on past Temple and Somerset House towards the Houses of Parliament, Westminster Abbey through Parliament Square to St James's Park. Turn and look back and see the Treasury and the Foreign Office divided by the statue of Clive of India. The Admiralty is to the left. This was once the epicentre of British imperial power.

Cross the Mall when the traffic has stopped at the lights. To the right is Admiralty Arch, to the left is Buckingham Palace, and in front is Lancaster House. Carry on up through Green Park to the commercial wealth of the West End, Mayfair and its hedge funds, Savile Row, Oxford Street, Selfridges – the first modern department store – then to Hyde Park, the site of countless demonstrations and protests.

It is a walk through thousands of years of history. London as a global mercantile city of bankers. The civic community that held its own against unruly monarchs. The unruly city of rioting apprentices and the London mob. The proletarian society that helped to make the English working class. Walk anywhere and England's history is there.

And there is also the dark side of London. The poverty, the hard times and the inequalities that have existed together, often in the same street but now starting to harden into zones of exclusion. It is

William Cobbett's 'great wen'. The anonymous, brutal city as machine that can crush the vulnerable and the lonely and shows little mercy.

But above and beyond all this, London is home. It is the countless small horizons of our everyday life – our local estate, our street and community, our neighbours, the local school. It is the everyday life of shops, clubs, pubs, parks, community associations and sport. We are an English multi-ethnic global city. We are parochial and international. Our personal family associations sometimes stretch around the world, sometimes no further than the next street.

All of this is embodied in London's mayor. A mayor for the people of London, if still not yet for the city of London. That must wait for another democratic revolution. A mayor to stand up for our interests. This book is about the politics of mayoralty. Its message is that we can break with the inertia of Westminster and Whitehall and do something popular and better and different with politics. That's been London's history. With London's mayor lies the possibility of injecting innovation into the torpor of our political system. A London that will give England and the UK a lead. Building partnerships with our other English cities to spread power around the country.

It is in this spirit of democratic renewal that Labour's manifesto calls for change in how we govern our country: 'Our governing mission is to break out of the traditional top-down, Westminster knows best approach, and devolve power and decision making to people and local places.' Our reasoning is simple: 'Labour believes meaningful and lasting change for the better is only possible when people are given the power to change things for themselves.'

So if you love London as your city and your home, please do read this excellent book. David is one of our city's great social innovators. Is the political class ready for this kind of radical democratic politics? It doesn't matter. Don't wait for permission or nothing will change.

Jon Cruddas
April 2015

Jon Cruddas was head of Labour's Policy Review 2012–15. He is also co-author of *One Nation: Labour's Political Renewal*.[1]

# CHANGING LONDON

This book is a rough guide for the next mayor of London, capturing the radical but practical ideas of the people of London and embracing a pioneering and collaborative approach to politics. It is the book the voters wrote – vital reading for those who would be mayor and those who will decide.

# ABOUT THE AUTHORS

The Changing London website is an independent project. It was set up by David Robinson and Will Horwitz to gather ideas for London's next mayor, and to debate them, develop them and promote them.

www.change-london.org.uk

David is a community worker and a father of three. He has lived in east London all his life and been involved in social change in lots of different ways, but mostly he has worked for Community Links (www.community-links.org), a charity he set up many years ago. David also co-founded Shift (www.shiftdesign.org.uk) and the Children's Discovery Centre (www.discover.org.uk). He can be contacted at

david.robinson@change-london.org.uk

Will has lived in east London for seven years. He has worked as a researcher and campaigner for charities including Oxfam and Community Links, and this year went back to university to study political economy. He can occasionally be found on twitter (@willhorwitz) or can be contacted at

will.horwitz@change-london.org.uk

# ACKNOWLEDGEMENTS

Some of the ideas here have been borrowed from other cities. Most began with posts on www.change-london.org.uk. We are grateful to all those who wrote blogs or comments, set up consultation meetings, contributed to start-up costs or helped with research material, creative work, promotion and publicity.

Thank you Aisha Chowdhury, Alex Pickup, Alisa Helbitz, Amir Jabarivasal, Andrew Attfield, Andrew Dick, Andy Hull, Andy Thornton, Anne Longfield, Anne Power, Athena Lamnisos, Becky Booth, Ben Kentish, Bharat Mehta, Caroline Middlecote, Catherine Sermon, Christian Wolmar, Clare Tickell, David Blood, David Christie, David Grayson, David Hutchison, David Lammy, David Wilcox, Deborah Hargreaves, Deborah Mattinson, Diane Abbott, Don Paskini, Eleanor Rosenbach, Ella Britton, Ellie Robinson, Emily Benn, Esther Murray, Frances Clarke, Gail Greengross, George Clarke, Giles Gibbons, Giles Piercy, Gill Hay, Glenys Thornton, Gracia McGrath, Graham Fisher, Holly Donagh, Jack Graham, Jack Stenner, Jacqui Howard, Jake Hayman, James Beckles, Jamie Audsley, Janani Arulrajah, Jane Tewson, Jessie Robinson, Jo Casebourne, Joe Cox, Joe Robinson, John Page, Jon Cruddas, Jon Miller, Jonathan Rutherford, Julian Dobson, June O'Sullivan, Karl Brown, Kate Jopling, Kitty Ussher, Konstantin Dankov, Linda Woolston, Liz Meek, Louise Bunce, Louise Winterburn, Lucy Parker, Mandy Wilkins, Marion Janner, Mark Ferguson, Matt Downie, Matthew Smerdon, Megan Jarvie, Michael Green, Michael Harris, Michaela Rhode, MsUnderstood Partnership, Neal Lawson, Nick Stanhope, Oona King, Ossie Fikret, Paul Hocker, Paul Twivy, Peter Baker, Peter Sebastian, Radhika Bynon, Ray Shostak, Richard McKeever, Robbie de Santos, Rosie Ferguson, Ruth Stokes, Sadiq Khan, Sally Goldsworthy, Sally Rogers, Sam Tarry, Sarah Holloway, Sarah Richardson,

Sean Baine, Sheyda Monshizadeh-Azar, Simon Chouffot, Stan Harris, Steve Wyler, Sylvie Bray, Tahseen Chowdhury, Tessy Britton, Tessa Jowell, Tim Jones, Toni Nash, Yvonne Roberts and Zoe Kilb.

Thank you all.

Some opinion poll data in this book is from unpublished quantitative analysis of the BritainThinks 2014 'Capital Gains?' research report and it is used with their kind permission.

# INTRODUCTION

London is a wonderful city, diverse and full of talents, but is it the best that it could be?

Almost 9 million people live here, alongside some of the world's most successful organisations. It is, in many ways, a rich and gifted city, but not always a happy, healthy or productive one. More than a third of its citizens fear crime on the streets, 28 per cent are in poverty, and the richest can expect to live twenty years longer than the poorest.

The London mayor holds the UK's biggest directly elected mandate. We should expect from them an ambition that matches the scale of the opportunity – it should be fair, deliverable, bold and, above all, it should be ours, not marketed to voters with badges and balloons in the four short weeks of an election campaign but imagined and owned by us all.

San Antonio's mayor ran huge live events for thousands of citizens to decide the city's budget. Bogotá's former mayor Antanas Mockus asked citizens to voluntarily pay 10 per cent extra tax, and 63,000 did. Oklahoma's mayor transformed his city's waistline by personally fronting a campaign to 'lose a million pounds'. Helsinki's mayor introduced a youth guarantee of a job, study or training place for every young person. And bike-sharing schemes are common now, but they were pioneered – in the face of widespread ridicule – by former Paris mayor Bertrand Delanoë. The list goes on. Mayors across the world have rocked their cities in recent years with extraordinary achievements. If they could do it, couldn't we?

The next mayoral election in May 2016 and, in particular, the primary contests to choose the candidates in summer 2015, give Londoners the opportunity to set a different agenda and to break new ground.

We set up a website in November 2012 and invited contributions. Changing London was to be a platform for generating and debating ideas, drawing on the experiences of other cities, but first and foremost on the creativity and innovation of Londoners. Thinking anew, not only about the direct responsibilities of the mayoralty but also about exploiting the powers of influence – the voice, the visibility and the unique capacity to convene that comes with the office. These are the superpowers of the mayoralty overlooked by policy brewed in Westminster and ignored in a feeble public discourse that fixes too often on political celebrity.

We didn't have to wait for very long. The ideas and the discussion flowed freely. This book brings it all together under five big visions for London: What would the city look like if we determined to make it the best place on earth to raise a child? Or if it was a friendly city, where neighbourhoods thrived and everybody mattered? How could we build a fair city where lavish wealth is as unwelcome as abject poverty and both have been eradicated? Or maybe a healthy city, that did no harm and tackled sickness at its source? And, to lead it all, how should we revitalise and retool a sham democracy that saw only 38 per cent vote in the last mayoral election?

Ideas range from play streets to plotting sheds, London Sundays to a Have-a-Go Festival, a London Fair Pay Commission, a Children's Trust Fund and a cultural guarantee for every child, Citizens Budgets, a Mayor's Share in the biggest businesses and the April Vote – an annual London referendum.

These and hundreds more are not a manifesto for the next mayor but a rough guide – a glimpse of how our city could look if we dared to gaze beyond the cautious consensus that has infected Westminster debate, and if we reclaimed the city as a place we share and build together.

The ideas here are bold – some might say idealistic – but they are not naïve. At the last mayoral election Boris Johnson was returned with the support of less than one in five Londoners. That leaves a lot of stay-at-home voters left to play for. They won't be reached with politics-as-usual. Our headline message to the mayoral wannabees assembling at the starting line is therefore unequivocal: fresh, engaging, innovative plans, building on the ideas and touching on the everyday interests of ordinary Londoners, would be good for London, good for politics and, potentially, very good for you.

But Changing London didn't start with mayoral candidates and it doesn't finish with them. We think the business of change is a concern for us all. We hope that the ideas here will inspire all our readers to do the following five things.

**Carry on imagining:** you will know what needs to change in London. It may be sparked by an idea in the book, or something you spotted yesterday, or it could be a plot you've been hatching for a while. Share your ideas on Changing London (www.change-london.org.uk) and read what others have come up with, too.

**Be heard at a hustings:** for the primary campaigns in summer 2015 and the election itself in spring 2016. Push the candidates and stretch them with the breadth of your vision for London and the standards you expect of our next mayor. Share the ideas in the book or ideas of your own.

**Do it yourself:** London isn't made by the mayor alone – anything but. Many of the ideas in the book could be made real in your neighbourhood, right now. Pick something and have a go – set up a play street or a community group, campaign for local businesses to pay the living wage, or, if you run one yourself, start paying it. Join something, start something. Do something.

**Hold the winner to their word:** twenty-first-century politics is synonymous with broken promises. If London's next mayor is going to be different they must start by sticking to their word. It is our job to make sure they do.

**Keep it up:** ideas can take time to germinate and even a superhero mayor won't be able to do everything in their first year. Persevere.

Martin Luther King Jr famously believed that change wouldn't come overnight but that we should always work as though it were a possibility in the morning. A website and a little book won't deliver the change we want, but ideas light the fuse. Share yours. Vote for yours. Work for yours. Rock this city.

# CHANGING·LONDON

# 1

# BECAUSE WE DWELL TOGETHER

Londoners awoke to the news on a damp May morning in 2012: Boris was back.

Less than one in five had voted for the sitting mayor but this meagre support was endorsement enough. His opponents had polled even less.[2]

Why did a city with, at the time, seventeen Labour-led councils and twelve controlled by the Conservatives[3] reject Labour policies and choose a Tory mayor and why, above all, did 62 per cent not vote at all?

The disinterest was surely not borne of contentment. London is a buzzing city of nine million souls but one in four are lonely often or all of the time.[4] Some of our families are extremely wealthy, but a third of our children grow up in poverty[5] and although our richest citizens outlive the Japanese, the healthiest nation on earth, our poorest have a similar life expectancy to the people of Guatemala, ranked 143rd.[6]

The questions that should have occupied progressive minds after that last mayoral election were brushed aside as attention shifted to the personalities that might participate in 2016. The cabals were reconvening, bloggers were blogging and the *Evening Standard*, and even the national press, was puffing out the gossip. Would Tessa Jowell run, David Lammy, perhaps, or Sadiq Khan?

With more than three years to go before the next vote, no one stopped to wonder: does anyone, beyond the faithful anorak, really give a monkey's? If not, why not, and what lessons can we learn before the game begins again?

# Our Rough Guide

Livingstone and Johnson are as interesting and as entertaining as anyone in British politics but they couldn't excite enough commitment to compel the weary majority to the ballot box. Plainly, big personalities do not, on their own, generate mainstream engagement.

We think the ground is won or lost between elections, not with tittle-tattle and intrigue, but with intelligent conversation that feels relevant to the people who could vote but probably don't. It's big ideas, not big names, that light the slow fuse of the possible.

That's why we launched Changing London in autumn 2013, with a tiny website and two ambitions. We wanted to gather suggestions for the next London mayor – practical ideas and the big vision – and we wanted to do it with a bottom-up approach to politics.

We didn't have a lighbulb moment. There was no dream and we didn't even have a plan, but we did have a hunch – a hunch that Londoners experiencing different aspects of our city might have ideas about how it could be better. We were interested in creating a 'warehouse of ideas' for the next mayor because, like Eleanor Roosevelt, we think that 'small minds discuss people, great minds discuss ideas' and that diminishing the issues belittles the electorate and fuels disaffection. We weren't backing a single candidate, we were backing the people of the city to put forward their suggestions for changing London.

And they did.

We set up a daily blog generating and debating those ideas and also drawing on work in other cities. We were especially interested in how the great change-making mayors across the world 'catalyse action and get stuff done' by exploiting so effectively the powers of influence that come with the office – the voice, the visibility and the unique capacity to convene.

Bruce Katz and Jennifer Bradley had published *The Metropolitan Revolution* earlier in the year.[7] 'Cities and metropolitan areas are action oriented' they had written, 'they reward innovation, imagination, and pushing boundaries. As networks of institutions they run businesses, provide services, educate children, train workers, build homes, and develop community. They focus less on promulgating rules than on delivering the goods and using cultural norms rather than regulatory mandates to inspire best practice. They reward leaders who push the envelope, catalyse action, and get stuff done.'

We shared numerous examples of the kind of stuff that Katz and Bradley were writing about: Seoul's mayor, former community activist Park Won-Soon, has launched a visionary programme to transform South Korea's capital into the world's first 'Sharing City'.[8] Boston's Thrive in Five brings together hundreds of teachers, social workers, parents and children to ensure every child is ready to start school at the age of five.[9] Stockholm aims to be the world's leading green city by 2030,[10] and Amsterdam plans to reduce its carbon emissions by 40 per cent by 2025.[11] The list was long.

For six months we posted hundreds of suggestions: Play Streets and London Sundays, a Have-a-Go Festival and a cultural guarantee for London's children, a Mayor's Share in the top 100 businesses, citizens budgets and an annual London referendum ... and so on and so on. Then we marshalled that material into themed papers and we organised events to discuss them. This book is the product. It is our rough guide for the next London mayor.

## THE MAYORAL SUPER POWERS

Over the past seven years, Mayor Johnson has become one of the UK's most recognisable politicians, deploying the bully pulpit to develop a profile far in excess of that warranted by his formal powers. Consider how worthwhile that might have been if only he had more to say that opened hearts and minds, that was constructive, healing, generous, collaborative, bold or inspiring. The mayoralty, we think, comes with a set of 'super powers' – a voice that is heard afar, a visibility that extends far beyond the official remit, and a unique capacity to convene people from across the city, the government and the world in the interests of London and Londoners.

Imagine switching on the news one evening and hearing the mayor, our mayor, saying:

I want to start a conversation. Our financial services sector is a vital employer, generating wealth and opportunity. We are proud to be world leaders but that means we must embrace the responsibilities of leadership. This is why I want to discuss the Robin Hood Tax – a tiny tax on global financial transactions. Hong Kong, South Africa and South Korea have found a way to do it. Couldn't we?

Or perhaps, picking up the *Evening Standard* and reading of a mayor, our mayor, making this case to fellow Londoners:

I refuse to call London a 'great city' while one third of our children grow up in families that are struggling. Poverty stems from the structure of our society and the rules of our economy: it is about the rich just as much as the poor. We need a more thoughtful approach to policy at the bottom. We also need a more thoughtful approach at the top.

The capital needs a leader who can inform public opinion and articulate an ethical argument, doggedly shifting the moral centre of the conversation. A mayor who will listen to and speak up for those whose voices are seldom heard and little understood.

The cautious consensus that infuses almost every 'debate' in Westminster is carefully calibrated for the swing voter who, apparently, abhors the different, the bold or the radical. It is not an approach that works for would-be mayors. The electorate has demonstrated a lively appetite for alternatives in its city favourites. Across the UK, and indeed throughout the world, mavericks have run well in mayoral contests, and neither Johnson nor Livingstone campaigned as figures of the establishment although both, with distinguished exceptions during Livingstone's first term, largely governed in prose.

What might this more radical approach look like in 2016? The rest of this book is full of examples and ideas but we highlight two here. At the Changing London Open Meetings, candidates and possible candidates talked a lot about children and a lot about inequality – two of our most significant themes – but they centred almost all their remarks around poor people and poor children.

This is easy but it is not nearly enough. A bold candidate would ask instead: how do we build a fair city, where power and wealth and opportunity are shared more equally? This is not primarily about working with the poorest, because the ugly inequality that is flourishing in London at present is manifestly not their fault. Children's centres and good schools and work experience are important, but so are a maximum ratio between the lowest and the highest paid, employees being appointed to company boards, a financial transactions tax to rein in the City, the end of speculative investment in London's housing, and much more. Similarly, a mayor with high ambitions for London's children wouldn't only have a policy prescription for its most 'troubled families' but a shared vision that applies to all of what it means to grow up a London child.

A healthy city, a fair city, the best city in the world to grow up – these are wide, inclusive ideals. Delivering them will call for big bold inclusive ideas and the strength of character to see them through.

Bill de Blasio had both. He came from behind to win the mayoral race in New York by exposing the widening gap in income and opportunity between the richest and poorest. He attacked the 'lazy logic of false choice politics … that those of us who serve can't expect to achieve anything at all if we dare to advance policies that are bold and morally right.'[12]

Brave? A certain gumption, perhaps, but other mayors have also shown the way. The mayor of Thessaloniki, Greece's second city, has spoken about the time when a quarter of the city's population were sent to concentration camps during the Nazi occupation. When a fascist Golden Dawn candidate was elected to the city council, the mayor wore a prominent Star of David on his chest at the swearing-in ceremony.[13] Mayors make news, news influences opinion, and opinion shapes behaviour, both amongst the movers and the shakers in the city and, ultimately, amongst the voters next time around.

In this context, deeds matter almost as much as words. In Chapter 5 we reference the overweight mayor of Oklahoma who led by example in a city-wide campaign to 'lose a million pounds'. Now, not only are its citizens thinner and fitter, but lower healthcare costs and diminishing workplace absentee rates have attracted unprecedented investment, unemployment is down and Oklahoma City boasts the strongest economy of any major metropolitan area in the US.

Canadian Naheed Nenshi became the first Muslim mayor of Calgary – indeed the first Muslim mayor of any major north American city – in 2010. The relatively unknown former management consultant snuck into office with 40 per cent of the vote in a field split by competing stalwarts of the establishment. He then surprised them all with his flagship project – 3 Things for Calgary (www.3things forcalgary.ca) – encouraging his citizens to imagine three things that they could do for their community and then to persuade three friends to do the same. Calgarians embraced the innovative approach with great enthusiasm and returned him to office for a second term with an impressive 74 per cent of the vote.[14]

A younger generation that is disillusioned with mainstream politics identifies with issues, not tribes. A same-old versus same-old contest in London in 2016 will not ignite the passions of an electorate that is young, substantially unaligned and increasingly bored – if not terminally disaffected – by business as usual. For mayors and would-be mayors, breaking new ground is very smart politics.

## A New Approach to Politics: Do or Die

'In this century, metropolitan areas, rather than nation states, will shape the world's social, cultural and economic agendas' says the international think tank the City Mayors Foundation.[15] City mayors don't have the power of prime ministers but nor do they have the constraints, or the distractions that come with that wider responsibility. When once threatened by an opponent who claimed to 'have a plan', boxing champion Mike Tyson replied 'everyone has a plan until they get punched in the mouth.'[16] So it is with national governments. Every new PM has a plan, then events fight back. City mayors are in a different ring, less affected by the unforeseen.

Changing London has focused on the areas where mayoral candidates have been short on ideas in the past. This isn't to say that bus fares and congestion charging and inward investment aren't important, they assuredly are, but we believe London needs candidates who think beyond the points of marginal difference.

We need contenders who raise the debate, leaders who inspire and stretch us all and push at the boundaries of the possible.

And without wishing to be too alarmist, we look at the figures from the last election and we look around us now, and we fear it's do or die.

For the last fifty years the mainstream parties have been haemorrhaging membership and core support as the big voting blocs based on social class have steadily declined. 'The mass membership parties of postwar Europe', says Nick Pearce, 'not only represented the political demands of their core constituencies, they helped to frame and organise their social lives and civic engagement... Voting for a party was not just a rational choice but an expressive act through which ties of loyalty and belonging were given meaning.'

'Increasingly, however, as the communities of social class fractured, parties came to lose these moorings. They became more professionalised and narrowly composed, with recruitment and promotion mechanisms increasingly focused on access to, and advancement within, the hierarchies of public office. As the realm of the state became more important, the special adviser took over from the shop steward.'[17]

This loss of identity and the consequential sense of powerlessness have contributed, according to Jon Cruddas and Jonathan Rutherford, to 'growing levels of anxiety, addiction, depression and loneliness. Problems that have a social cause are experienced as humiliating personal failures. Individuals are left alone to cope with these problems as best they can and public services treat the poor like supplicants and victims.'[1]

Politics and politicians no longer provide the answers or even offer hope, something to believe in. Add in the expenses scandal and an apparently ever-increasing disappointment in the conduct and integrity of people in high places, top it off with some deeply divisive policies like the Iraq war, tuition fees and the deficit-reduction strategy, and it is unsurprising to discover that public support for politicians has never been lower: just 18 per cent of the British public now have any trust in the people who govern us.[18]

Inevitably, people stop voting or they find a party that appears to represent something completely different. Immigration dominates the agenda, 'refracting voters anxieties' say Cruddas and Rutherford, 'into a brittle politics of loss, victimhood and grievance'. A positive political discourse is displaced by blame and recrimination. Romanians, benefit claimants and single parents, 'troubled families', young people, old people, teachers and social workers are variously offered as the scapegoat. 'Brittle politics', small minded, self-serving, mean spirited and unattractive. So it is that party members find better things to do and voters look away.

Changing London is very small, but within this tiny initiative there are the seeds of an approach that has the potential to better serve a large and diverse electorate and to reinvigorate democracy for a new generation.

Our contributors aren't mindlessly happy but they are optimistic. They recognise very clearly the challenges and the problems in this city at the moment, but all of the ideas here are about making London better in the future – anything that was just a whinge did not make it onto the blog.

Clement Atlee famously believed that Labour won the stunning victory in 1945 because 'we were looking to the future. The Tories were looking to the past.' Similarly, our contributors believe it is by dreaming new dreams that we improve the lives of Londoners, rebuild interest in the political process, and win the mayoral election in 2016.

## A Time for Ideas

Two wider developments make this a particularly timely moment for crowdsourcing and debating new ideas for the next mayor.

First, the Labour Party has introduced selection primaries for members, registered supporters and affiliates to choose the standard bearer. At the time of writing it looks likely that the opportunity will attract at least half a dozen candidates and probably more. It also seems probable that the other main parties will adopt a comparable process. A faithful and undifferentiated incantation of the Westminster line on every issue won't enable anyone to stand out from the crowd. Bold distinctions will be debated, refined and selected or rejected. Ideas will be needed.

Second, devolution will be a major point of discussion in both the selection process and the subsequent election. As cities and regions across the UK pitch for enhanced powers, London has so far been unconvincing in its response. Specifics are thin on the ground, and at the moment it is only a bullish sense of entitlement that seems to unite London politicians, commentators, lobbyists and cheerleaders.

The deal for Greater Manchester, the first in the wake of the Scottish referendum, gave the mayor control of a new housing investment fund, enhanced planning powers, increased responsibility for local transport, welfare-to-work programmes, existing health and social care budgets, business support and further education and up to £30 million a year from the Treasury in recognition of the extra growth – and tax revenues – that Manchester will generate.[19] It's a big deal for the city.

So why Manchester, some Londoners wondered, and not London?

At a meeting shortly after the Manchester announcement the responsible minister, Greg Clarke, supplied the answer with visible exasperation: 'Manchester came to me with a plan for what they would do with more power' he said, 'Londoners keep telling me why they are entitled to more power. That doesn't wash.'

Nor should it, and if the discussion hasn't gathered substance by the time of mayoral selections and elections it must do then. Our next mayor needs to earn new powers. They need a plan for London that inspires popular and cross-sector support and that demonstrably merits government approval. Once again, they need big bold inclusive ideas.

Here are ours.

# CHANGING LONDON: THE HEADLINES

There is much to admire in London, but it isn't perfect. Our city tops the tables on 'technology readiness and economic clout' but is way down on health and fairness and work–life balance.[20] Leading is good but ensuring that no one is left behind is even more important. An explicit commitment to fairness and equity has been a running theme in the Changing London discourse.

We live in an age of new technologies disrupting and changing relationships and behaviour. An internet sensibility infects all that we do, online and off. We expect customised service and user involvement. Changing London has been less about what the mayor can do for us – we no longer trust the promise anyway – and more about what we, with the right mayor, can achieve together.

These principles – fairness and equity, voice and agency – have underpinned our conversations and are the load-bearing poles of a big and popular tent. Within this framework we imagine a mayor with three distinct approaches to their work.

First, they would inquire and listen, inspire and explain, convene and provoke, engage and collaborate.

Second, they would prioritise a little light institution building. Ideas need vehicles to carry them forward, and we're not looking for short-term projects but serious commitments with enough investment to embed them in the landscape of our lives.

Third, they wouldn't stop talking about the big vision – the best place in the world to grow up, a fair city or a healthy one, these are big visions – but nor would they miss the strategic power of the local initiatives that can catalyse wider change. There are times when social acupuncture can be more effective than monolithic bureaucracy.

This book isn't meant to offer a step-by-step political programme for the next mayor any more than a rough guide for travellers offers a coherent itinerary for a lengthy expedition. It is a set of practical suggestions rooted in real-life experience. We have imagined London as a great place to grow up, as a neighbourly community where everybody matters, as a just city where power, wealth and opportunity are fairly shared, and as a healthy place where sickness is tackled at source.

And we have imagined how we might achieve the changes we are calling for in a deeper and revitalised democracy.

Of course these approaches aren't mutually exclusive. A good place to grow up would also be safe and healthy, a fair city would also look after its children, ensuring that none are left behind, and a place where neighbourhoods thrive would be fertile ground for strong local democracy and civic engagement. The sum of the parts, a clutch of modest ideas and a few big ones, would change for good the political narrative in London and transform our capital city.

## A GREAT PLACE TO GROW UP

In the next chapter we imagine how the next mayor might make London the best place on earth to raise a child. We suggest a set of six rights promised to every London child, including a fun and friendly neighbourhood, the extra help whatever it takes, and the first steps into a good career. Ideas include the introduction of 10,000 Play Streets, building on a 'presumption of consent', a Cultural Guarantee of the things we will have experienced by the time we leave school, an overarching strategy for the elimination of illiteracy, an annual 'Have-a-Go Festival' and a London Child Trust Fund so that all enter adulthood with some savings to their name.

## A CITY WHERE NEIGHBOURHOODS THRIVE AND EVERYBODY MATTERS

In Chapter 3 we reflect on how the places where we live, and the relationships within those places, shape the quality of our lives, and we imagine a city where neighbourhoods thrive and everybody feels important. Ideas include using guidance and regulation to design social connection into the places where we live, not design it out; introducing the Danish concept of a 'Right to Space' for community activities and adopting a 'social acupuncture' approach to seeding new projects; driving the colocation of local services with a London Register of Public Assets; establishing a Co-Production Academy; and openly measuring social progress with a London Index.

# A Fair City

In our fourth chapter we tackle fairness and equality and imagine a city where power, wealth and opportunity are in the hands of the many not the few. Here we suggest four guiding principles.

**On poverty:** having enough to live on should be an entitlement in a rich city, not a privilege.

**On wealth:** remuneration distorted beyond the dreams of avarice is no more useful here and no more welcome than abject poverty.

**On business:** businesses of good character are defined not by shareholder return or contribution to GDP but by the difference they make to the lives of Londoners.

**And on housing:** houses in London are for people to live in and there must be enough for everyone. They should no longer be treated as investment vehicles.

Ideas include a Mayor's Share in London's biggest businesses, a London Fair Pay Commission, a Mayor's Pledge adopted by 'businesses of good character' to pay fair wages and fair taxes, and – like the mayors of Nantes and Brussels – active mayoral support for a tax on financial transactions.

# A Healthy City

We look at a city that prioritised the health of its citizens and imagine the programme of a mayor tackling sickness at source in Chapter 5. To promote healthy communities he or she should tackle inequality, clean the air, make it easier and safer to cycle and walk, outlaw smoking in parks, and ban fast food outlets near schools. Tackling mental health stigma, introducing traffic lights on restaurant food and learning about first aid, cancer, diabetes and how to keep fit in an annual Save Ourselves Week would ensure that we all have the knowledge to stay healthy.

## A Deeper Democracy

Chapter 6 takes a different approach. Whilst earlier chapters have been about what the mayor might do, this one focuses on how they might do it. It's about effective leadership and retooling democracy in London for the twenty-first century. 'Ideas for London' would be the new permanent City Hall agency charged with seeking out and developing new ideas. An annual April Vote would see Londoners take part in a referendum on a big issue facing the city. Citizens budgets would give us a say over how our money is spent, and a Table for London and a London Calendar would provide the infrastructure around which we settle the really difficult issues, decide on priorities and work together on improving the city we share.

## A Spirit of Can Do

If there was a single continuous thread in the many and diverse contributions to Changing London, it was a spirit of can do. We don't like everything we see but we do think change is possible.

We are bewildered and even alienated by the vision often repeated by mayoral wannabes – 'the world's most competitive city' – partly because, as one contributor at our open meeting pointed out, it raises the question: competitive at what? Ballroom dancing, quiz nights, drinking games? But mainly because it has so little resonance with the average Londoner. Although 77 per cent of London residents are proud to live here only 17 per cent believe that they benefit from the building development in the capital.[21] Big-shot London – big offices, big salaries, big business – is relatively peripheral to most of us, and 75 per cent say that there are a lot of things that they would like to do in London but simply cannot afford.[21]

A winning candidate would understand that reality, and develop a promise for the next mayoral term that owed less to the Westminster playbook and more to the people of London. We have ideas, we believe they are practical and we think they would reach the parts of the electorate that others never reach

As Boris Johnson is now stepping down and Ken Livingstone isn't running again, the next mayoral election will be contested by first-timers. They have the chance to be something different, to stand for something more. It is very likely that they will be well-known, experienced, national politicians with a reputation to think about. Big ships are safest close to port but it isn't what they are built for. Though caution might be understandable it would also be a wasted opportunity, for London and for politics.

One of west London's most distinguished residents, T. S. Eliot, once asked:[22]

*When the Stranger says:*
*'What is the meaning of this city?*
*Do you huddle close together because you love each other?'*
*What will you answer? 'We all dwell together*
*To make money from each other'? or 'This is a community'?*

It's not a simple either/or – choices in government rarely are – but it is about priorities, and contributors to Changing London were unequivocal: we want candidates who know what matters most, leaders who will listen to Londoners and, in 2016, a mayor who will embrace fresh ideas and a new approach to politics.

# 2

## A Great Place to Grow Up

'If we can lead in finance (or law or fashion or Olympic Games) it is neither illogical nor grandiose to demand of our mayor that this great world city leads the globe in nurturing our young. It would require vaunting, breath-taking, ridicule-risking ambition.' So said south London teacher and community organiser Jamie Audsley, in one of the first contributions to Changing London.

Dozens of contributors shared Jamie's passion. They included children and young people, who mourned the paucity of sweetshops and the cost of games consoles but were forceful in demanding decent schools, better transport and housing, more to do, reduced inequality and more opportunity; in this their views differed little from those of our adult contributors.

London can be a wonderful place to grow up. Some can take advantage of the opportunities to learn, to play, to experience culture from all around the world, living in safe communities with supportive neighbours, good services, and a loving family. Yet low pay and high costs consign a third of children to living in poverty.[23] Densely packed, often-poor-quality housing damages health. Cars dominate public space, leaving little room to play. Insecurity and transience stop neighbours getting to know each other. Violence and fear blights the lives of a minority. We are a young city – a quarter of us are aged under nineteen – yet we don't want to grow up here: a poll asked Londoners where they would rather spend their childhood if given the chance again, and most opted for elsewhere.[24] Asked if London was a good place to bring up children, only 39 per cent of

15

people in the poorest areas said yes, compared with 81 per cent in the richest.[21]

The former mayor of Bogotá Enrique Peñalosa said:[25]

> We know a lot about the ideal environment for a happy whale or a happy mountain gorilla. We're far less clear about what constitutes an ideal environment for a happy human being... If we can build a successful city for children, we will have a successful city for all people.

He is right. Our infrastructure, services and systems are not designed with the happiness of children and young people in mind. They leave many desperately struggling to thrive, and it is to them that a civilised society must turn first. It also traps many in a childhood that is good but not the best it could be, and even the luckiest children would see their lives improved if the streets and communities around them were thriving too.

## THE RIGHTS OF EVERY LONDON CHILD

When they are growing up we expect a lot of our children and young people. In return they should expect more from us. In her contribution, Ellie Robinson suggested a set of expectations each child and young person could demand of their mayor and their city: the rights of a London child, spelt out because many are denied them at present. Based on the contributions to Changing London we propose six.

    (1) For every child: a fun, friendly community.

    (2) For every child: experience of all London has to offer.

    (3) For every child: the extra help, whatever it takes.

    (4) For every child: the first steps into a good career.

    (5) For every child's family: a decent income and a good home.

    (6) For every child: the right to be heard.

There will be many other ideas and more to add but we will know we have succeeded when the next generation are able to say: 'These are the birthrights of a London child; the best place on earth to grow up.'

# (1) For Every Child: A Fun, Friendly Community

## Ten Thousand Play Streets – and a Presumption of Consent

In 1972 a group of children living in central Amsterdam decided to reclaim their street from cars. With a calm, playful resolve they set up barriers at either end, organised petitions, took on irate car drivers and world-weary adults. 'Impossible! You cannot ever close a street! Out of the question!' said one. He was wrong. Local leaders took notice, they began rerouting traffic away from residential neighbourhoods, and introduced a 30 km/hour speed limit. Eventually the young campaigners won the right to a permanent play street, which still exists today.[26]

'Playing out' was a fond childhood memory for several of our contributors, but it barely features in the lives of today's children. 'For us it was fresh air, friends, games. For our parents it was a community, an excuse to chat, a sense of shared responsibility,' said Sally Rogers. Christian Wolmar recalls 'inter-war pictures where residential roads, with barely a car in view, were the site of a multitude of activities, ranging from women gossiping and cleaning the pavement, to children playing cricket or football on the cobbles.'

A bucolic vision perhaps, a victim of modernity. Not necessarily. In the 1930s children played on every street but cars were already taking over: the Street Playground Act of 1938 was introduced after thousands of children were killed in road accidents. It allowed local authorities to close residential streets between 8.00 a.m. and sunset. At their peak there were 750 around the country but by the 1980s most had disappeared. Until 2011, that is, when a group of parents in Bristol decided to use legislation intended for street parties to close their road for the day. Their play street was such a success that they set up Playing Out to support other parents in their efforts, and there are now hundreds around the UK, including many in London, after a campaign led by London Play and local residents' groups.[27] Once a week, or once a month, the street is closed to through traffic, with a few volunteers ensuring that residents can drive safely in and out.

At first glance play streets don't seem to deal with the tough stuff that should surely concern a mayoral hopeful: crime, transport, housing, health. A nice-to-have, perhaps, but a priority?

Yes. We think, a priority.

Public space in which to meet and play is the lifeblood of a thriving community, particularly for our children. Parks and playgrounds are vital but, astonishingly, roads make up 80 per cent of our public space in London.[28] We have surrendered them almost entirely to the car. Some are major trunk roads where cars undoubtedly belong but most are the local, residential streets along which neighbours used to meet and children used to play.

This affects our environment and our safety but also our community life. Pioneering studies as far back as the 1960s have shown that roads with more cars have fewer community activities.[29] Busy streets mean fewer chats over the front wall, fewer impromptu gatherings in the road, and fewer children playing out and drawing adults in. It is no coincidence that cul-de-sacs sustain the highest levels of social cohesion.[30]

These community relations themselves might seem inconsequential but – as the next chapter explores – the strength of our ties to friends and neighbours is vital to our health and happiness, our graduation rates, our chances of being a victim of crime and even our IQ.[31] Close-knit, supportive communities are core to the 'tough' challenges mayors grapple with.

Play streets bring another health benefit too. When originally introduced in the 1930s they were intended to prevent children dying in traffic accidents. Today we have evolved different responses to the same problem – the TV screen and the computer console – which have themselves caused a different kind of health crisis. Some have linked rising obesity levels to the decline in spaces to play.

Play streets are not difficult to implement: a barrier at either end of the road, a few volunteers to keep things in order, perhaps a few games to play with, and the children will do the rest. Legally very little stands in the way – as the trailblazers in Bristol, Hackney and elsewhere have shown – although there are legislative changes the mayor could make that would ease the process. Richard McKeever suggested a 'presumption of consent' whereby local authorities would have to justify to parents why a street could not be closed once a week or once a month if there was local enthusiasm for it to become a play street.

We suggest that 1000 new play streets could emerge in London within the first year of a new mayoralty. At around thirty per borough, it is not unachievable: Hackney has nearly twenty already. Within a four-year mayoral term sights should be set even higher: Angus Hewlett suggested a minimum of 10,000 – about five per primary school and enough that most children would have a chance to take part. Sally Rogers suggested every borough could have a Play Street Activator, driving the adoption of play streets within their local authority.

Using the voice and visibility of the mayor to engage local councils and encourage willing volunteers, the campaign would draw heavily on the knowledge and enthusiasm of groups like Playing Out and London Play, who are pioneering the resurgence.[32] The barriers are not financial or legislative but cultural and practical – exactly the kind that a bold, visionary mayor can take on and tear down.

## Redesign Public Space around Children

Play streets redesignate existing space but there is also scope to redesign it from scratch, particularly in new developments. Rotterdam's pursuit of its status as a child-friendly city required new or redesigned neighbourhoods to meet four criteria.[33]

(1) Child-friendly housing: specifications including a room for each child, a minimum amount of floor space, communal play areas and safe access.

(2) Public space: a set of development requirements that include, charmingly, 'a pavement suitable for playing, 3.5 metres wide on at least one side of the street, preferably on the sunny side' and 'trees with seasonal variation'.

(3) Child-friendly facilities: including at least one 'extended school' per district, which provides services and activities for the whole community.

(4) Safe traffic routes: with a child-friendly network of streets in every neighbourhood.

Because local government in Rotterdam is highly localised, the city government offered each district a 'scan' of their neighbourhood, assessing compliance with the four criteria and suggesting changes that could be made, on the understanding that the district would endeavour to implement some of the ideas. Many did. The programme cost €15 million in total and ended in 2011, but its legacy lives on in actions that districts are still taking to make their areas more child friendly.

London's mayor could use his or her planning influence to encourage and support the adoption of similar standards across the city. Progress might be incremental and it would take many years for the impact to be felt in every neighbourhood but, if adopted now, it would shape the city in favour of children for decades to come.

## Ban Advertising Near Schools and Playgrounds

In 2006 the mayor of São Paulo banned all outdoor advertising. Fifteen thousand billboards were taken down, store signs were shrunk, ads were taken off buses and leafleting was forbidden. Nearly $8 million in fines helped enforce the ban. When first proposed it was met with incredulity but eight years later it is still in place, and São Paulo is not alone – Auckland, Chennai, Vermont, Maine, Hawaii and Alaska all have restrictions or bans. Paris reduced its advertising by 30 per cent and prohibited it entirely within fifty metres of a school gate.[34] Grenoble has recently decided not to renew its contracts for advertising displays around the city.[35]

Advertising is so ubiquitous in London that it can be hard to imagine the city without it. More importantly, why would we? São Paulo billed their ban as an effort to clean up a cluttered and messy cityscape and London would benefit from this too, but there is a more important reason.

As Neal Lawson has written, 'Adverts are not there to inform but to sell one thing: unhappiness. They work because they make us dissatisfied with what we've got or what we look like. They make us want the next new thing, until of course the next new thing comes along.'

Their impact on children is widely acknowledged, with restrictions in place on advertising manifestly unhealthy products like alcohol and tobacco. But even adverts for seemingly harmless products exert the pernicious effect that Neal described. By marking out those who can and cannot afford the latest trainers, advertising turns inequalities of income and wealth into stark markers of social status.

Whatever we think of this in adults it is surely unjust that children are judged by other children according to what their parents can afford. Even a small step to lessen the influence of our acquisitive culture on London's children would bind us together from a young age. As a first step, the mayor could agree with London councils to ban all advertising near to and within schools, as has been done in Paris.

Children will be exposed to adverts on television and the internet and in the rest of the city but this measure would send a message and set a trend; our children deserve to live in communities unsullied as far as possible by the inequality for which they bear no responsibility.

## (2) For Every Child: Experience of All London Has to Offer

### London Sundays

Who first thought of covering themselves in silver foil, standing very still, and then moving just a little bit? And what made them think of it?

Two questions which must have occurred to many of us when wandering along the South Bank past the live musicians, magicians, jugglers, escapologists and those peculiar human statues. Not all to our taste, of course, but you don't have to stop and it costs no more than you think it is worth.

So an afternoon's free entertainment? Well no. The relatively short distance from, say, east London to the centre is the price of an off-peak travelcard, which can top £8 per adult: not insignificant for a family on a low income. So it is that even central London's free delights – the museums, galleries, parks and river walks – are seldom enjoyed by many outside zone 1.

As Sally Goldsworthy has noted, 'London is a leading cultural city with world class galleries, museums and theatres. Yet for many Londoners they remain undiscovered, more likely to be visited by tourists than a teenager from a poor background growing up in zone 4.' For a tourist a gallery is little more than an afternoon stop but for our children these experiences can open doors and open minds: 'For some it's jumping the highest, running the fastest, for others it's singing, dancing, painting, performing. For every child, a dream,' said Ellie Robinson.

Holly Donagh reports on research from charity A New Direction, which found that over half of young people in London hadn't been to a theatre performance, gallery or music event in the last year. When asked, young people say they want opportunities to be part of something, leading and decision making as well as simply watching; more free experiences 'that you just come across'; to be able to find out about what is happening more easily and get support to develop talents; and to see more arts in schools.[36]

The mayor of Bristol has been Making Sundays Special once a month: closing the centre of the city to cars, importing climbing walls and bouncy castles and inviting street performers to take over. Last year a giant water slide constructed down a main street attracted 100,000 applicants for 360 tickets.[37]

London saw something similar in 2012 when the Olympics and the torch relay that preceded it brought families out into London in force, congregating in person and in spirit around one of the world's great sporting events. London boasts some of the world's greatest cultural institutions all year round, which – with the right support – could recreate something similar and more permanent. We could start with one Sunday each month.

These London Sundays would see a coordinated programme of free events and activities designed specifically for young tourists from within the M25, widening access to London's art, culture, history and traditions. One Sunday could see the South Bank Centre or the Natural History Museum or the Tate lead a day's celebration beyond their walls. Others could feature some of London's best musicians, dancers, authors or poets.

To ensure everyone can take part, particularly in activities in the centre of the city, that tube ticket would have to be covered: a free return trip for every adult accompanied by a responsible child would remove one severe restraint on participation and open the event to every family.

The Olympics was a sporting occasion that opened eyes, inspired, drew Londoners together and briefly transformed our city. We can recreate the effect on a smaller scale, but regularly and consistently, once a month, with free tube and bus travel and some enthusiastic arts partners.

## A 'Have-a-Go Festival'

Edinburgh is world famous for its wonderful annual festival, but our participation is largely as audience members, watching others perform. Could London add to its fame by being the first to host an annual festival where we all take part? Act on the stage at the National, sing at the O2, play at Wembley, paint at the Tate, write at the British Library. Have a go at riding a bike for the first time, at learning to swim, at ballroom dancing, at healthy cooking, at being a first aider. For a couple of weeks every summer the 'Have-a-Go Festival' would see London's organisations, large and small, opening their doors to the public, particularly children, encouraging us all to join in.

Some museums already do this once a year, through an annual countrywide Takeover Day organised by charity Kids in Museums, which puts young people in charge of major cultural venues for twenty-four hours.[38] Employers in the public and private sectors could participate too, giving children the chance to try being a fire fighter, a city trader, a nurse, a plumber, a lawyer, a builder – or even at being a mayor. Opening doors and opening minds. Some opportunities would necessarily have to be restricted to only a few children but all should be advertised openly and for some activities there would be no limit on numbers.

A small central resource would provide a coherent brand and collate the opportunities in a programme and on a website, but individual organisations would be responsible for managing their own involvement.

A Have-a-Go Festival would not just open up new opportunities for millions of children but would send a message: London – its art and culture and sport, its community organisations, its best employers and its government – is here for the benefit of all its citizens, not just the tourists, the privileged few or those in the know.

## A Cultural Guarantee for London's Children

London Sundays and a Have-a-Go Festival would see children accessing the art and culture for which London is famous, but we could strengthen our duty further. Sally Goldsworthy argued in her contribution that the mayor should institute a cultural guarantee to all London's children, of things they will have had the opportunity to achieve by the time they leave school: 'For example, see a play, visit an art gallery, write with an author and be mentored by a professional artist. This wouldn't be a restrictive Ofsted tick box of fifty things to preserve but a dynamic list created by children, parents, teachers and artists that captures London's quality and innovation.'

Holly Donagh wrote: 'London schools currently have access to £450 million a year in funding through the Pupil Premium, and whilst this must support a range of needs for lower income pupils it could also fund cultural activity when it is clear that it helps in the development of those young people. All schools in the city allocating 10 per cent of Pupil Premium for cultural provision would help break the link between family income and cultural engagement and be one way of funding the delivery of a citywide guarantee.'

Alternatively, the scheme could be funded by the kind of Visitor Tax that is applied in Paris and New York. A one or two per cent levy on hotel bills would hardly be noticed by the tourist but it would be hugely beneficial to the children of London if spent in this way.

A scheme of the sort Sally and Holly describe – embedded across London's schools – would perfectly embody the agenda we describe. The mayor should lead its development and be the public face of its implementation. London Sundays would be a part of it but the educational infrastructure would help ensure no child missed out.

## Expand the London Curriculum

Credit where credit's due: the current mayor's education enquiry proposed creating a London Curriculum that weaves the history, culture and stories of London into English, art, music, geography and history lessons. It was launched last year, to great success. Holly Donagh suggests it should be expanded across the Key Stages, particularly to Key Stage 2.

She wrote about Kuopio in Finland, where each year of school is based around a different 'cultural path' – drama one year, film the next, dance the year after, and so on.[39] Dallas's Big Thought Arts Partners coordinates cultural education across the city, providing a portal where schools can view and book cultural experiences for their young people.[40] Mocca in Amsterdam run a city wide programme of training, online offers and discounts for schools on cultural experiences as well as advice and guidance for teachers.[40] And, closer to home, the World Heritage Organisations in Greenwich (The National Maritime Museum, the Royal Observatory and the Old Royal Naval College) have created a curriculum for Greenwich schools based on their local area.[41]

## (3) FOR EVERY CHILD: THE EXTRA HELP, WHATEVER IT TAKES

Sylvie Bray mentored a seven-year-old boy who had never been out of Peckham. When they took a Thames Clipper down the river he thought they were leaving the country. Sylvie could empathise more than most – parental domestic violence and alcohol abuse meant she was in care as a child. This is why we should listen particularly hard when, writing on Changing London, she said: 'Every child deserves the same chance to live, and to thrive. It's not acceptable that we just keep a whole group of children treading water … it would be terrible to give up on these kids.'

For some children, growing up in London is a dangerous, bewildering and painful experience. Some have parents who are unable or unwilling to look after them. Others might experience terrible difficulties at school, with mental health problems or with bullying. Research among children at the charity Kids Company found that one in five had been shot at and/or stabbed, and half had witnessed shootings or stabbings in the last year.[42] For many more the deprivation might not be as extreme but it is almost as debilitating for their future success: leaving school unable to read or write well enough to get a job, caring for parents or siblings instead of learning or playing. If our 'every child' ambition is to mean anything, it must extend most actively to the most vulnerable children: every child, from whatever beginning, with whatever it takes.

## A London Children's Challenge

By the early 2000s it was widely acknowledged that children were being badly let down by the poor quality of London's schools. In response, in 2003 the government introduced a new minister to take responsibility, some new money and a crack team of officials in the Department of Education to lead a programme called the London Challenge. Ten years later, with London's schools amongst the best performing in the country, the London Challenge is still hailed as a model of successful intervention.[43]

It focused on improving leadership and teacher quality but in doing so recognised that schools thrive when the staff and leaders feel trusted, supported and encouraged. It built partnerships between schools, often pairing better- and worse-performing schools, which actually improved the performance of both. It built on the belief shared by teachers and local authorities that no child in London should be let down by their school.

In short, a fantastic programme that transformed education for a generation of Londoners. Its only limitation? Children spend most of their time out of school. A great education can help overcome the effects of poverty or neglect at home but is no replacement for preventing them in the first place, and for some children it will never be enough.

Nowhere has recognised this more famously than New York's Harlem Children's Zone. Fed up with the duplication, gaps and inconsistencies in the myriad of public and philanthropic services trying to cater for children in the 100-block area of Harlem, its founder set out to weave them together into a coherent 'pipeline' from cradle to career. Schools were vital but so were charities, local care services, and parents and families themselves. Several organisations have attempted to bring the approach to the UK, including Only Connect, via their West London Children's Zone, and Save the Children. The model cannot be imported wholesale – services and jurisdictions are different – but the principle of joining up services in a 'doubly holistic' way, across all ages from 0 to 18 and across all domains, can be replicated here. Save the Children have laid out in detail how to transfer the model to a UK context, emphasising the involvement of local leaders, particularly local authorities and schools, and a robust governance structure.[44]

Perhaps we could learn from the best of the London Challenge and the Harlem approach. A London Children's Challenge would extend the challenge model beyond schools to the coordination of wider services for children, particularly those in the most disadvantaged areas. It would combine expert advice with peer support and some resources to bring together different services, similar to that which Save the Children has provided for some areas under their Children's Communities programme. Led from City Hall and adopting the same positive, supportive tone (in contrast to much of the rhetoric around child protection, which operates in a climate of media intimidation and political fear) it would champion not just schooling but the wider protection and support of London's children.

Other cities have shown how heavy investment in the lives of struggling children can pay off. Boston's Thrive in Five initiative aims to ensure every child is ready to start school aged five; it has brought together agencies and organisations across the city to create 'ready families, ready educators, ready systems and a ready city'.[45] San Antonio has pursued a similar goal under its SA2020 plan,[46] as has Hartford with its Mayor's Cabinet for Young Children – a cross-sector group of public sector, charity and business leaders in the city, appointed by the mayor. They provide high-level policy recommendations for the mayor and oversee budgets for programmes that serve young children across the city.[45]

In Cincinnati, an ambitious programme called Strive brought together over 300 city departments, charities, businesses, universities and schools to improve all aspects of services for children from cradle to career. They re-imagined the system piece by piece; performance improved across a vast range of measures.[47]

Learning from this experience, the mayor should champion four vital issues for London's children

## Eradicate Illiteracy

The *Evening Standard* launched the Get London Reading campaign in 2011 with the news that one in four children left primary school unable to read properly.[48] This campaign and others have gathered huge momentum since then but too many children still leave school unable to read and write well enough to thrive in adulthood. In West Dunbartonshire, renowned child psychologist Tommy Mackay has shown that it is possible not just to tackle illiteracy but to eradicate it.[49] We should seize the opportunity and aim for the same in London, redoubling our efforts and, following Mackay's lead, setting out to change attitudes as well as provide one-on-one support for those who need it most.

The 'Read On. Get On.' campaign is demanding that by 2025 all children leave primary school as confident readers. Led by a group of charities, teachers groups and publishers, it is avowedly a community campaign, arguing that this cannot be a job for government alone.[50] The mayor's high-profile support could propel it forward in London.

## Every Child Mentored, Every Child a Mentor

Several contributors to Changing London outlined the enormous benefits of mentoring schemes for children who 'do not know about their city or, even worse, are afraid of it' and for mentors, who experience a whole new side to London. Gracia McGrath challenged the next mayor to become a mentor himself, to 'see the city through the eyes of a child'.

Extending this theme, Ellie Robinson argued that 'having a mentor can transform a childhood – building confidence, extending networks, eroding inequality' and wondered whether we could extend these benefits across the capital through a voluntary mentoring scheme in every school. Crucially, children would have the opportunity to be trained as mentors and to be mentored themselves, because giving support is just as valuable as receiving it.

Some children will need far more than a mentor alone can provide, but establishing it as a right would guarantee every child a minimum of one supportive, trusted relationship, and a role providing the same for others when the time comes.

## Shrink the Foster Care Waiting List to Zero

Mentoring could be for everyone but fostering is mercifully rare. How we care for children whose parents can't or won't care for them is a defining feature of a civilised society and yet, as Mandy Wilkins pointed out, there are over 1000 children in need of foster care in London and not enough willing carers.[51]

A concerted campaign could see the fostering waiting list reduced to zero by the end of the mayoralty. We should allow ourselves no leniency – in a city of 9 million people it is not unreasonable to believe we can find families for 1000 extremely vulnerable children.

Marjorie Fry once observed 'You cannot give a child love by act of parliament'. Nor can you by mayoral decree, but Mandy's piece concluded with some very practical ways in which City Hall – leading by example – could champion fostering amongst its own employees:

active promotion, time off to go through the assessment and training, flexible working. Then she suggested that 'the mayor should use his or her voice to encourage other public, private and third sector employers to follow suit, as has been done with the living wage campaign'.

## Coordinate Child Protection

Even better would be to prevent children needing foster care in the first place. Matthew Downie outlined some of the specific challenges London faces in protecting our children: 'gang violence and sexual abuse within gangs; abuse of children through belief in spirit possession and witchcraft; and the problem of mobile and transient families where children at risk of abuse move frequently and easily across the city.'

He goes on: 'The prevalence and seriousness of the issue commands political attention across local and national government, but so far not from either of the two mayors of London. Why not?'

We could, he says, learn from successful programmes in other cities, like New York's Blue Sky programme or Manchester's co-commissioning of children's services across multiple local authorities. It is a complex topic with no easy solutions, but throughout this rough guide we talk about the importance of influential leadership, about the mayoral super powers, the voice, the visibility and the capacity to convene. Nowhere could these be better applied than on this agenda, making the case over and over again that enabling every child to succeed means 'every child' from whatever beginning, with whatever it takes.

## (4) FOR EVERY CHILD: THE FIRST STEPS INTO A GOOD CAREER

### A Youth Compact with Business

A ten-year-old in our children's discussion group in east London suggested schools make better links with banks so he and his peers could better understand how to work in one.

It is sobering to learn that work experience and the worry of getting a good job should feature in a child's concerns alongside the availability of fizzy drinks. But it is also a sign of just how important access to the right job can be for children and their families.

For a minority of our children, the path from school to college, perhaps to university, and then on to the first rung of a good career is well paved, assisted along the way by good schooling, inspiring work experience, family connections and perhaps an unpaid internship or two.

For others the transition into work is difficult and traumatic, often unfulfilling and sometimes impossible – unemployment amongst under-25s in London stands at 25 per cent.[52] With young people arriving in London from all over the world, the competition for jobs at this level is fierce.

The first step is to discover what is out there. Sally Rogers described how, 'When children from working class families in places like Newham grow up and – aged fifteen or sixteen – are sent off for a couple of weeks work experience … they end up spending two weeks stacking shelves in Shoe Zone. These kids – far more than their rich contemporaries – need experiences of work that inspire and excite. Two weeks shelf stacking won't do that.'

Changing London contributor and local councillor Jamie Audsley, along with a group of young people in Croydon, has set up #FirstStepCroydon to campaign for better work experience. Working with Croydon Citizens and Teach First, the campaign has already won promises for 200 work experience placements, with expenses, from a huge range of local businesses, charities and public sector agencies.

Unpaid internships for many of the top professions exclude those who cannot afford to work for free. Informal advertising of entry-level jobs is a further bar to those who haven't had access to the internships and don't have the family connections where these crucial networks are built up.

Instead, too many find themselves stuck in insecure, temporary, badly paid jobs with no training and no path for promotion or advancement. Apprenticeships traditionally provided a sure-fire route for those who didn't go to university, and there has been a recent re-vival in interest, but there is far more a dedicated mayor could do.

Public sector employers are already beginning to lead the way. An-drew Attfield reported on Barts NHS Trust, for example, which offers apprenticeships to local residents, including into new areas such as operating theatres, pathology labs and the outpatients department. He observes, 'if the NHS can do this at a time of great pressure on its services, other sectors should be able to do so much more'.

Much of the responsibility for delivering on this agenda lies with employers but a mayor exploiting the influence their position brings could encourage, cajole and coerce. Setting the agenda with a few of London's largest employers could transform the rest.

The mayor could establish a Youth Compact with Business, setting the expectation that responsible businesses would do three things for young people starting out in their careers.

(1) Provide meaningful work experience in non-entry-level jobs for young people from local schools. The number of placements could be a fixed proportion of their number of employees, or could be re-lated to their turnover.

(2) Offer apprenticeships in an ambitious range of roles for young people, particularly those local to the area where the employer is based. Again, the number could be in proportion to the size of the organisation.

(3) Only offer internships that are fairly recruited, with fair remu-neration of at least the minimum wage, and clear contracts, and sign up to Intern Aware's Fair Internship Charter.[53]

A driven mayor would have a range of tools at their disposal. Di-rect influence over parts of the public sector would mean the police and Transport for London could blaze the trail. Other public services, including the NHS and local authorities, could be quickly signed up, particularly because many meet these criteria already. They could be extended to companies contracted to provide public services.

Writing on Changing London, Jake Hayman and Amir Jabarivasal suggested that every college and secondary school have a staff mem-ber dedicated to supporting former students in finding a career: 'Their job would be to source opportunities for work experience, insight days, internships and even jobs, to organise CV/interview clinics and have drop-in careers counselling services.' Many students maintain strong connections to their school or college, and even those who haven't done so might be more likely to return there for the support than seek it at the Jobcentre. £100,000 would be enough for the initial scoping, with a further £750,000 needed to pilot it.

As for private sector employers, Chapter 4 covers the mayor's relationship with business. We argue that a thoughtful mayor with a campaigning mindset and a willingness to engage provocatively with businesses could skilfully convene and cajole around some core themes. A Mayor's Pledge would set out our expectations of a good London employer. It would include the opportunity to take those vital first steps into a decent career.

If necessary, institutions could be built to help promote these aims, including, for example, a London Interns Service advertising decent opportunities and allowing participants to rate employers, or an Ofsted-style mechanism for holding employers to account in how they support young people into work, as suggested by Jamie Audsley and Emily Benn.

In addition, local control of the BIS training and skills budget would help to ensure that this important resource is directed towards the areas of deepest need and greatest potential, not least, perhaps, helping with this locally specific institution building.

## (5) For Every Child's Family: A Decent Income and a Good Home

An astonishing 37 per cent of London's children live in poverty: their parents trapped by low wages, insecure and insufficient jobs and high prices.[54] Our status as 'child poverty capital of the UK' should be a source of acute shame for a city that has much else to be proud of.

For a mayor who has little direct influence over wages or benefit and tax rates that directly affect income this can seem at first glance a hard problem to tackle. One approach is to make income matter less. Opening up public space, banning advertising near schools or increasing access to the arts means that a child's experiences are less dependent on their parents' income. Kate Bell has called this a process of 'de-commodifying' the experience of childhood: narrowing the spheres in which family income determines a child's life chances.[55]

But a visionary leader does more than mitigate the effect of gross inequality. New York's Bill de Blasio won his mayoral election by exposing the pernicious effect of the gap between rich and poor on one of the world's few other Western mega-cities; it will surely feature equally prominently in London's upcoming vote. We touch on some ideas below and develop more in Chapter 4.

## A London Child Trust Fund

The UK government's Child Trust Fund was set up in 2005 and has been described as 'the most successful savings scheme there has ever been'.[56] On the birth of a child, parents were entitled to claim a small payment from government into a ring-fenced bank account, which they could then add to. In a few years' time that first generation of newborns will turn eighteen and gain access to the accrued savings. Assets which – research suggests – are vital for a successful transition to adulthood. Sadly, the impact will be short lived; the scheme was cancelled in 2010.

But in the meantime, something similar has been launched by San Francisco's mayor Gavin Newsom just for his city.[57] Under the 'Kindergarten to College' programme, every child starting kindergarten receives $50 in a special bank account ($100 for children receiving free school meals) to be used to help pay for the costs of college when they reach eighteen.

It acts as seed funding; under a deal between the city and some of its biggest corporations, private sector contributors then match any additional money put into the account by parents or the child themselves, up to $100. Another $100 is added if people enrol for monthly deposits. The city and private contributions are reclaimed if not used for college-related expenses before the child reaches 25, but people keep any family contributions. Fully launched in 2012, the accounts now reach 8000 children, with 4700 opening each year.

Mayor Newsom has proved that where government won't step up, a city leader can. We have some of the world's biggest corporations in our city – there is nothing stopping a ground-breaking partnership of this kind taking off here. On its own a London Child Trust Fund will not transform our city overnight, but it will endow the next generation of Londoners with vital assets with which to begin their journey.

## Support for Childcare

Parents and children need stable, high-quality, reliable care. This isn't cheap. Full-time childcare in London costs £14,000 per year on average,[58] which goes some way to explaining why employment rates for women with children in London are 12 per cent lower than the national average.[59] Government helps a bit for working parents but still leaves a lot for parents to cover, creating very difficult choices for the lowest paid. Women step out of the labour market with all the attendant long-term disadvantage as well as the immediate hit to the family finances at precisely the time when they need all the help they can get.

National support for childcare is vital and the mayor should make the case particularly vehemently for London, but perhaps the mayor could offer some more direct help too, by setting up a Childcare Loan Fund with London's financial institutions, with patient and sympathetic repayment terms over twenty years or more, with payments suspended or cancelled in times of illness or unemployment and eventually waived completely. The Social Market Foundation suggested a plan for a national equivalent in 2012.[60] This isn't ideal in what is now a heavily indebted economy but, for better or for worse, we are accustomed to borrowing and a fair, long-term scheme similar to student loans might be a way forward for some parents.

Meanwhile, Anne Longfield pointed out that even setting aside the finances, childcare can be difficult to access and poorly suited to jobs outside the nine-to-five. She suggests more work from the mayor to provide information to parents and better coordinate existing services, as well as stimulating new more flexible provision.

**Higher Pay for the Lowest Paid**

We consider poverty and inequality in depth in Chapter 4 but its particular impact on children deserves special mention here. Londoners know all too well the costs of bringing up children in the UK's most expensive city. The London living wage is set by the Greater London Authority each year as the minimum hourly income needed to get by, and yet one in five workers is paid less than its current rate of £9.15 per hour. Both London's mayors to date have been enthusiastic supporters of the living wage, and 400 employers – including the GLA – are now formally committed to paying it, but as the current mayor admits, there is a long way to go to reach his target of the living wage being 'the norm across the capital' by 2020.[61]

As Megan Jarvie argued, mothers are less likely to work in London than in the rest of the country, which goes some way to explaining high levels of child poverty. The high costs of childcare and housing and the lack of well-paid, part-time jobs all stand in the way. Almost half of part-time workers earn less than the living wage, so a strong focus on improving earnings in these jobs would disproportionately help families.

Meanwhile, with a quarter of London households now renting privately,[62] secure rental contracts would immeasurably benefit children who can settle in a school and a community instead of suffering disruptive moves at short notice at the whim of exploitative landlords. More social housing would stop families being driven into the private sector in the first place. And, as Robbie de Santos argued, more homes for middle-income families would stop communities fragmenting as new parents are forced to move far out into the suburbs to afford housing.

**Financial Literacy for All**

The charity Action for Children found last year that 45 per cent of children and young people had not received any financial education at all. This hits hardest those without strong family support, often forced into managing precarious finances from a young age.[63] Being able to confidently negotiate savings, bills and loans is, perhaps regrettably, a vital part of modern London life. The mayor could lead the various players in this, the financial centre of the world, to eradicate financial illiteracy. Schools, colleges, banks, businesses and institutions like the Bank of England could all play a role.

## (6) FOR EVERY CHILD: THE RIGHT TO BE HEARD
### A London Young Mayor

'Young people tell me constantly that they want to be part of the solution to the challenges facing London – not seen as one of the problems,' said Rosie Ferguson in one of the first contributions to Changing London. 'Yet there is a disconnect between young people's intrinsic passion for changing things and their ability to connect and see relevance to formal political structures; and this is why they are angry.'

In Chapter 6 we will look at how we can ensure that London's democracy is a thriving, continuous process of engagement rather than a tediously formulaic ritual every four years, and harnessing the ideas and energy of children and young people will be at its core.

But the idea of allowing those under sixteen the chance to elect their own representative is an obvious first step towards introducing a greater say for children and young people – the only group currently denied any formal say in the running of our city. Young people may be electors in waiting but they are citizens now.

Child Mayors and Young Mayors are increasingly popular around the country, including in several London boroughs, but we propose a small twist: restrict the vote to those aged under sixteen but allow candidates of any age to put themselves forward. After all, children and young people should be able to elect the person who they think best represents their views, irrespective of age. It is the exclusion from the democratic process of those aged under sixteen, not the age of the person elected, that deprives children of a voice.

Leeds has a Child Mayor, introduced as part of its bid to become a child-friendly city. Year-six pupil Charlotte Williams gained thousands of votes for her ideas, including getting more people cycling to coincide with the Tour de France's visit to Leeds in 2014. The city's child-friendly efforts began when they asked thousands of young people how the city could be improved and then distilled the answers down to twelve wishes. Top of the list were safe ways to get around the city and creating a centre that's welcoming, safe and with plenty to do.[64] Charlotte led the charge.

A London Mayor for Children and Young People would represent the views of all those aged under sixteen in City Hall and more widely. They would have a significant budget and take on or share responsibility for those parts of the mayor's portfolio concerned with children and young people. They could be scrutinised by a panel of children and young people, perhaps including the young mayors of those boroughs which have them.

Four years is probably a reasonable term of office but a long time in the life of an adolescent. We therefore recommend that the panel is granted a right to recall the youth mayor and hold a fresh election if a significant majority feel that the selected candidate is no longer serving the best interests of the capital's younger citizens

## LAST WORDS: A GREAT PLACE TO GROW UP

Politicians often talk about children but rarely outside of the services that national ministers are charged to deliver: schools, child protection, childcare, Sure Start. When they speak they may be sincere and knowledgeable but they talk about services or they talk about small groups of the most deprived children and their families – those who need the extra help – as a problem to be tackled rather than participants in the political process.

What they rarely, if ever, do is describe their vision for family life in London. The London mayor can tell a new story, not forgetting schools and social services but not limited to them either; weaving a vision that includes streets and parks, businesses and charities, housing and income, art and culture, participation and learning. He or she can lay out a vision rather than promise a set of services, and they can use their status to draw others in, challenge them where necessary and together craft a different city.

This is just one possible vision but we think it is powerful and ambitious: a city reoriented around our children, guaranteeing the next generation a set of rights for which they could hold us to account. A great place to grow up.

# 3

# A City Where Neighbourhoods Thrive and Everybody Matters

## Where People Belong

'London is where important people live', we were told by a nine-year-old in Silvertown.

'We live in London!' said her friend.

'Then we must be important,' replied the first.

It's easy to feel the opposite in a big city – insignificant, overlooked, unimportant. Some Londoners have neighbours, friends, family providing all the support that they need, but one in four feel lonely often or all of the time.[4] Ten percent feel lonely every day.[21] We want to live in a place that we love and we want to be loved in the place where we live. A place where people are friendly and generous. Not in an in-your-face, happy camper kind of way but in a neighbourly and supportive way. It makes us feel better: safe, strong and more capable.

We don't want to be unnoticed. The stories of people dying alone, unseen for days, offend our common humanity and it scares us. We know that some people who live in London, particularly in the centre, are just passing through for part of their lives or part of the week, but most of us aren't. We belong here and have a right to be seen. We have a part to play, however small, and want to be wanted. We have a voice and a right to be heard. These are the simple reciprocities, the give and take, of a place where people belong.

We believe that politicians can make a difference and that a good mayor could help to fashion a city where everybody felt important, but we know that others are less positive. Perhaps Londoners are disenchanted with politics because mayoral 'big visions' often seem remote from our everyday lives. We feel that our concerns, even though they might touch the lives of many of our fellow Londoners, don't much matter to the people in charge, and nor do we.

London is many things but most of all it is home to the 9 million people who make it work and who choose the mayor. Weirdly, politicians and their advisers, often in thrall to Westminster orthodoxy but remote from voices on the ground, miss the screamingly obvious. Contributors to Changing London have been very clear about the central issues: it's the people, stupid.

Alvin Toffler said, 'You've got to think about big things while doing small things so that all the small things go in the right direction.'[65] We would express it differently and say we cannot achieve the big things we want for London if we do not attend to the small things first.

Great places are made from the particular and it is the smallest parts of this big city, the communities where we live and the relationships within them, that shape the quality of our lives.

This chapter is about what the state does and how it does it, it's about what we as citizens do and how we do it, and it's about the relationships between state and citizen.

A good mayor would lead the planning and development of London in ways that make it easier to connect. They would encourage participation in the design and delivery of services and they would stimulate and support the programmes that bring people together and can catalyse wider change. We picture a city of thriving neighbourhoods, places we can get our arms around and where supporting one another is a natural part of everyday living. We imagine togetherness and community spirit right up there with red buses and Big Ben as the first things we think of when we think of London.

Don't be fooled. As political ideas go this one is a TARDIS. At first glance it looks small and insignificant, but look around inside and you realise it's enormous. We are interested in exploring the neighbourly city as the galvanising goal for the next London mayor not because the local bonds and little bridges are more important than, say, policies for tackling poverty, reducing crime or improving health but because we know that almost four times as many people find work through friends and neighbours than through Jobcentre Plus.[66] We know that stronger neighbourhoods have significantly less crime,[31] that loneliness is twice as deadly as obesity[67] and that living in a supportive community increases our chance of good health by 27 per cent.[68]

In short, we are interested in the quality and quantity of our relationships and the strength of our local communities because these factors significantly determine economic and educational performance, local crime rates, long-term health and much else besides. Attention to the individual, to the local, is not an alternative to a big vision; it is the making of it.

## A SENSE OF SELF

Giles Gibbons wrote on Changing London in the opening week[69] that, 'when I ask my friends in London where they live they don't say London, they say Hackney, or Clapham, or Marylebone – that's the thing about London. It's not one city at all, it's a ragbag of villages glued together...These different areas really do feel unique and have a sense of self to them... If we're going to release the enormous power of Londoners to be the engine of change for the city we need to enable it to happen in the villages.'

'Villages of London' was a recurring image but not one that all our contributors recognised. Clearly some areas have the 'sense of self' that Giles described and some Londoners experience it, but there is a way to go in others. We know it can't be spread by diktat from City Hall or anywhere else but we believe it can be seeded and nurtured, obstacles can be removed, progress evaluated and good things grown.

## FOUND IN THE CROWD

Chicago's mayor Rahm Emanuel says 'some things I can do and some things I can ask for'.[70] Similarly, the London mayor has some direct powers that could be better used to support and develop local communities – planning for instance – and some things they can ask for.

The moral exercise of influence, not control, is a challenge to the modern political role model in the UK but if politics is failing in London, then politics must change. We will be electing a leader for London in 2016, not a president or even a chief operating officer. Good leaders, as Maya Angelou observed, 'see greatness in other people',[71] and wisdom, as we discovered through the daily blogs on Changing London, is to be found in the crowd. 'The test of the next mayor's radicalism will not be the agenda they dictate' wrote Neal Lawson on the first day of Changing London[72] 'but how effectively they empower the people of London to collectively transform our city.'

## FIVE JOBS

The suggestions that follow in this chapter are occasionally radical but essentially practical. They are also tentative and in some cases totemic – they illuminate a set of approaches that could have many applications. We suggest that the next London mayor should apply a combination of the structural levers and those powers of influence to five big jobs.

(1) Connect by design: plan and provide for social connection.
(2) Sow the seeds: stimulate community activity strategically.
(3) Focus close: lead the transition to truly local services.
(4) Champion the willing citizen: recognise, motivate and inspire replication.
(5) Learn to improve: measure our progress and learn as we go.

## (1) CONNECT BY DESIGN: PLAN AND PROVIDE FOR SOCIAL CONNECTION

In the late 1800s policymakers began to realise that designing and building homes, streets and public places with due regard to sanitation and public health had a direct impact on the fitness and wellbeing of the nation and especially on its economic productivity. A series of public health measures were enacted that were radical at the time but which today we take for granted.

We know that the built environment also influences the way we interact with one another and therefore affects our mental well-being as much as our physical health, but still planners in the UK largely ignore this dimension. The parent of a primary school child, for example, knows how their local network expands and improves when they join the school gate fraternity. A peer network evolves sharing knowledge and, often, practical help. Just as the school gate brings together people with common interests and concerns so too do allotments, places of worship, local shops, outdoor markets, cul-de-sacs and even shared dustbins. We can design social interaction into the places where we live or we can design it out.

## Plan for Connection

The next London mayor should plan for connection, ensuring that the development of the physical environment facilitates personal interaction and doesn't impede it. Such guidance and regulation on the social plumbing is already in place in other countries. Ignoring it in this great modern city should be just as unthinkable for planners, architects and builders – and just as illegal – as ignoring the need for water pipes and sewage mains.

As we suggested in Chapter 2, play streets are one example of how streets could, from time to time, be used differently for shared activities that are community led. Street parties and garage sales, mentioned later in this chapter, are further examples.

Retaining the customary purpose of the street but consciously exploiting every opportunity for community connection is also important. A mayoral candidate already looking for a legacy could do worse than invest in 30,000 benches – roughly fifty in each ward but prioritising the predominantly residential. Thirty thousand Street Seats risk cheap parody, but observe how the very occasional bench in residential estates is already used to see how this most basic and practical item of street furniture facilitates connection. The benches might even be 'christened' by a local school, shop, GP surgery or place of worship. They wouldn't sponsor them in the usual way but they would name them after a well-loved teacher, neighbourhood street sweeper or health visitor. Our 'Bob's Bench' would be so much better than a 'Mayor's Chair'.

Ruth Stokes pointed out that 'high streets are not just about commerce; they're places where people meet and eat, and they provide a community focal point when often there isn't a viable alternative. We need to keep them as places where we want to be, and places that offer choice.'[73]

She suggested that local loyalty cards, like the Live Love Local card, could help to sustain flourishing high streets, and she proposed the extension of the local currency movement:

The Brixton Pound[74] is the first to take root in a London borough... Shoppers exchange their pound sterling for the currency, and they've then got a ready-made incentive to shop in local stores accepting the currency. The shops signed up to these schemes will also often offer their own incentives, such as discounts, so consumers get something back. Brixton has launched a 'pay by text' option to make the currency more accessible... The mayor could also tap into a national initiative supported by the British Independent Retailers Association. MyHigh.St[75] brings together the benefits of shopping locally with the convenience of shopping online, offering national delivery from local shops. It has a feature allowing users to 'discover' high streets, showcasing what a particular area has to offer in the way of independent shops. Consumers earn 'hi points', which they can spend at a later date through the website, and businesses get point-of-sale materials, a web presence and an online community focal point.

This is just a handful of examples of how a good mayor might help to change the ways in which the city configures, supports, controls and develops its roads, its schools and public amenities, its housing estates and its open spaces. Facilities whose primary purpose is not to facilitate wider social connection but which sometimes do and sometimes don't depending on their design and management and which, importantly, always could under a new mayoral commitment to planning for connection.

## Shared Spaces

'Thriving neighbourhoods', wrote Tessy Britton,[76] 'need shared community spaces. Shared gardens, canteens, kitchens, and work spaces can become the focus around which communities become socially, economically and environmentally sustainable. From a Sewing Room in Amsterdam, to HackerMoms in the US, the Reading Room in Rotterdam, The Common Room in Norwich, MakeSpace in Cambridge, Men's Sheds in Australia and across the world – people are creating spaces that bring people together to share ideas, grow projects and ventures together and shape their local community as part of their everyday lives.'[77]

London, Tessy says,

> has some shining examples of community-led spaces but they are rare and outnumbered by empty or underused facilities... We charge old age pensioners room rental for the smallest activity – and at the same time worry about their isolation and accompanying health effects. If the financial sustainability of a community space is entirely dependent on its rental income – rather than being viewed as a whole-system tool, as catalysts for creating outcomes and value in the community – more and more will shut as cuts work through the system.

Local councils in Denmark pay community associations for the costs of rooms and facilities wherever a community can demonstrate a level of interest in any given activity.[78] This kind of 'right to space' would be a paradigm shift from the conventional applicant/supplicant relationship between councils and community groups here in the UK but it could be transformational and could be achieved in London with the establishment of a modest fund for covering the cost of community spaces wherever the interest can be evidenced.

## Plotting Sheds and Building Blocks

Some might argue that social clubs are hardly the stuff of serious politics. Contributors to Changing London disagreed:

'Political parties and business networks are stuck in industrial-era models of accountability in a digital age that is increasingly powered by the informal and ad hoc' argued Julian Dobson.[79] The sensibility is changed by the technology but, crucially, it doesn't stop there. Expectations are raised. The Facebook generation expect to be involved, to 'generate content', to be seen and heard in every aspect of their lives. These expectations must be realised offline as well as on. The next mayor will meet that challenge or, as we are already beginning to see, lose that generation.

Julian suggested that the mayor should provide 'visible and high-profile forums where ordinary citizens can put forward and develop ideas to improve the capital ... where the people are, not in the formal surroundings of City Hall or town halls.'

He proposed Plotting Sheds in our major high streets: 'spaces where people can drop in and find out what's going on, have their say on new proposals and get together with others to develop ideas of their own ...spaces where the informality of social networking can meet the needs of locality and the creative energy of face-to-face contact. The plotting shed would bypass the gatekeepers who too often ensure that good ideas are smothered by bureaucracy or turned into political footballs. Each "shed" would be a welcoming, informal and politically neutral space, created at minimal cost – for example, by using temporary leases on empty shops – and staffed by a community organiser whose role would be to facilitate conversations, develop ideas and inform local people.'

The facilitator would be responsible for summarising ideas put forward by 'plotters', submitting them to the mayor, local authority or business owner as appropriate, and then sharing the response. The mayor would fund and support the network, protect its non-partisan ethos, ensure that each suggestion received an appropriate reply, and hold organisations to account if they didn't.

Successful communities are, of course, largely dependant on the people in them but the built environment significantly determines how we connect with one another. It is a paradox that we live on top of one another but so many feel lonely, more than anywhere else in the UK. There is no shortage of people in this crowded city but we do want for human connection. Planning and providing for social connection with the smart design, development and use of the public realm are the literal building blocks of a thriving neighbourhood, places with a sense of togetherness where everybody matters.

**Now Let's Pause a Moment**

Planning for connection, a Right to Space, a London pound, Bob's Bench, Plotting Sheds! Would any serious politician with a design on high office dare to walk this way? We think they should, not despite the fact that these approaches are unconventional, but precisely because they are.

If we want to live in a city where everybody matters, one that better meets our needs, that has the audacity to imagine and the capacity to deliver, and if we want to own that city, play a part, speak and be heard, we need a London mayor who won't just do the same thing over and over again and expect different results.

Our city of thriving neighbourhoods needs inward investment, good buses and effective railways, decent employment opportunities and clean air and all the kinds of things that we expect to concern our elected leader. And it needs radical new approaches to the building and sustaining of relationships and to the development of places we can get our arms around. These are not alternatives to delivering the citywide fundamentals but nor are they incidental. A good mayor would do both.

So hold tight and we'll carry on.

# (2) Sow the Seeds: Stimulate Community Activity, Strategically

Nick Stanhope drew attention to the importance of opening our minds to new and different ways of building communities: 'There has been a lot of work done on the role of churches, libraries and community centres on social capital and every bit is valid, because these are unequivocal sources of mutual support, interaction and civic participation. They are cornerstones but every policy, project and product affects social capital in some way, from Twitter to Jobcentres, and we should understand all these influences and how to harness them.'[80]

The Local Government Information Unit found that 74 per cent of the 8.5 million people attending a 'Big Lunch' event in July 2012 now feel a stronger sense of community, and 80 per cent feel closer to their neighbours.[81]

Andrew Dick suggested[82] that London might learn from the success of these kinds of events and try another approach to community building. The Australian Garage Sale Trail manages to make waste management fun and engaging, and like the Big Lunch it leaves an enduring legacy: 'Created in May 2010 as part of a local creative community festival in Bondi, Australia, the idea of organising coordinated garage sales on a single day was a huge success. It won awards and generated so much interest that in April 2011 it went national and, by the following year, some 150,000 people participated across the country, selling items at an estimated value of $2,471,513 and creating an estimated 45,084 new neighbourly connections in just one day.'

It's a simple idea: gather up the old toys, the unwanted presents, the books you'll never read again and stick them on the pavement. Sell for charity, recycle, meet the neighbours. Big Lunch founder Tim Smit says street parties are the 'excuse we need' to connect with one another. It's not the sandwiches that matter. It's permission to speak. The Garage Sale Trail is something similar.

These 'new and different ways of building communities' are essentially platforms for making connections, no different in principle from the school gate or from Facebook but playing to very different audiences. That diversity of appeal is very important.

Other contributors to Changing London suggested street dances, pavement drawing (Richard McKeever[83]), learning projects like The U (Radhika Bynon[84]) and even jokes in the bus shelter. It wouldn't be surprising if a putative mayor looked down this list and did what politicians invariably do: pick an idea, find a pot of money and promise a programme. Then, a launch and a lunch and a logo later, one short-term scheme emerges, flutters around for a few years and disappears.

None of these ideas would be bad ones to flutter on their own but they should be part of a strategy. The successful mayoral initiatives that have transformed other cities succeeded because they articulated a big ambition, animated it with practical initiatives and then very actively helped many flowers to bloom.

## A Thousand Flowers

Visitors to the Olympic Park in 2012 enjoyed the stunning beauty of wild flowers growing along the banks of the waterways and in other beds. It was a bold and inspired decision to eschew the formal, ordered beds of most municipal parks but it would be wrong to imagine that the Olympic beds were just allowed to grow wild. Seeds were sown, plants were tended. There was an overall plan; a coherent strategy that encouraged diversity and nurtured the natural. The cultivation of our neighbourhoods should follow this model. Plan the strategy, know what you want to achieve. Start with what comes naturally, sow seeds, support growth and allow 1000 neighbourhoods to bloom.

The Barcelonan architect Manuel de Sola Morales coined the phrase 'urban acupuncture' to describe something similar.[85] He was talking about the process of using urban design and small-scale interventions in the built environment to transform the larger urban context. The next London mayor should understand the potential for this kind of approach and practise a kind of community acupuncture with a Strategy for 1000 Flowers: vigorous strategic support for the local initiatives that both build platforms for neighbourhood connections and that can catalyse wider change.

This probably calls for a simple grant scheme to seed those initiatives as well as a thoughtful approach to nurture and spread them. For the most part we have tried to avoid ideas on Changing London that conclude with the simple recommendation 'spend money'. It can be too easy to say and too difficult to do, but let's put this one in perspective. Seeding 1000 'flowers' – community-led initiatives dedicated to the development of thriving neighbourhoods at, say, £1000 each – would cost £1 million. The total annual social and economic cost of mental ill health in London is, according to the GLA, £26 billion.[86]

We can see the potential of this 'acupuncture' approach by reflecting on a different policy area. Asked to name the most significant achievements of either of the first two mayors, the so-called Boris Bikes were amongst the top three most common answers in our straw poll. Today, as everyday, more than twice as many trips will be made on the number 25 bus running past my door as on all the Boris bikes. Last year the bikes accounted for 9.5 million journeys, the number 25 for 20 million and the entire London bus network for 2335 million.[87]

From these figures you might conclude that the bikes are actually an insignificant part of London's transport strategy, just as an annual street party, for instance, might seem peripheral to changing London, but that would miss the wider point.

The bikes have attracted attention and focused it on the joys of cycling, the dangers and the potential. The scheme may not yet be very big but it has changed our understanding of transport needs and opportunities in London, it has helped to move our thinking, to shape the terms of the discussion and, potentially, to reimagine transport planning for the future. A relatively small-scale intervention, well publicised, has significantly influenced the wider context.

Two phrases in that last section should be emphasised: 'strategic support' and 'catalyse a wider change'. We began this chapter with the argument that 'the quality and quantity of our local relationships significantly determine economic and educational performance, local crime rates, long-term health and much else besides'. Serious stuff, worthy of a place at the top of a mayoral agenda, but we know that none of that inevitably flows from random, short-term initiatives unconnected to a wider strategy. Window boxes down the high street can help to build local pride and community spirit but sometimes they are just boxes with flowers in.

Stanhope again: 'London's mayor should focus on profound influences within communities, rather than the superficial layers that can sometimes be mistaken for the same thing. If many civic values have drained out of communities over the last fifty years ... then we can't pretend that they can be replenished overnight with overtly contrived initiatives and short-term projects. Let's ask how we can establish permanent sources of mutual support, civic participation and associational life that grow slowly and become self-sustaining influences within their communities.'

And let's open our minds to the idea that that 'self-sustaining influence' could be almost anything that is, crucially, led by, for and with the local community – a neighbourhood market, an annual event, a local Facebook group – starting with what comes naturally, sowing seeds and supporting growth.

Two summers on, the wild flowers in the Olympic park are not contained in tidy rows or identical beds but they are stronger and more beautiful. True leaders plant trees or, at the very least, perennials.

## (3) FOCUS CLOSE: LEAD THE TRANSITION TO TRULY LOCAL SERVICES

We've noted that we now expect a richer, deeper, more personal experience from the services we use and that we want to share experience, knowledge and ideas, to generate individual content and to constantly communicate. We have recognised that what began with technology doesn't stop there and that the internet sensibility is infecting the real world of physical communities, relationships and services. At the moment public services in London cater adequately for many but can't reflect our differences or embrace our contribution. They are good at transactions but not at relationships. The next London mayor must recognise the implications of this momentous shift in social attitudes and behaviour and help to realise its benefits for the development of public services in the city.

They should assist, inspire and, where possible, require commissioners to deliver truly local services, and they should encourage and enable all Londoners (and especially service users), to participate in the design and delivery of that provision.

Writing on Changing London, Louise Winterburn described the prevailing management approach to most public services as 'scale and standardisation'.[88] Citing Locality and Vanguard research she put forward several reasons why 'local by default' should be, wherever possible, the cultural expectation of our public services in London and the new operating principle.

Economies of scale may work for the making of widgets but support for the clinically depressed patient, the desperate parent, the isolated elderly person works best at a local level. The 'big is always best' approach lacks the granular sensitivity to maximise efficiency on tackling issues that are definitively personal and it ignores and squanders the assets of the wider community.

Louise suggested that managers and purchasers should assume that local is always best unless and until the evidence proves otherwise. What matters, she argued, 'is not size but knowledge of context, and that can only be obtained on the ground'. Services should be commissioned in ways that 'help people to help themselves. Current services focus on needs rather than strengths. Human-shaped services build on strengths and promote responsibility instead.' This requires a 'focus on purpose, not outcomes. Predetermined output targets start from the wrong place. Effective interventions find out what people need and ... manage value, not cost.'

## Neighbourhood Companies

Giles Piercy went further.[89] He suggested that

> most deprived communities, or at least those that are heavily dependent on public services, feel 'dependent' rather than in control of a service. We need to find a way to generate far more local democracy and one of the ways to achieve this would be to create more local democratic organisation with control over budgets and tax raising.
>
> Public sector providers need to have a fundamentally different conversation with communities. Rather than spending lots of time asking them 'how would you like us to spend your money?' which tends to be at the heart of community engagement, they should start from a completely different stand point such as: 'Are you aware that we spend £xxx million collecting waste from this community? If you were able to persuade the community to move to communal bins we would give you £xx million to spend on whatever you want.'

'We've worked out that between the council and local health organisations we spend £5 million a year providing care and community nursing services. Do you think there is any way that the community could do aspects of this better and cheaper than us?'

Giles suggested a cohort of neighbourhood companies – locally owned and community led public service delivery agencies each focused on their local patch.

## Community Budgets

Such companies could lead to, or be the product of, a process of community budgeting. Citizens budgets allow residents of whole cities or parts of cities to propose ideas and then vote on how to allocate some spending. In Poznan, citizens have voted to fund a new shelter for homeless people, new bike lanes in the eastern part of the city and the renovation of a sports complex.[90] Versions of community budgeting have been tried in the UK but have mostly involved tinkering on the margins of the big budgets. A much bolder approach would be a borough decision, not the London mayor's, but it would be useful to have a leader in City Hall who raised these possibilities, shared experience from further afield and encouraged a London-wide movement towards thriving neighbourhoods with a deep and genuine grip on their own development. We explore this further in Chapter 6.

## Co-Production Academy

Gill Hay argued[91] that 'involving people through co-design or co-production processes can contribute enormously to good services. Involving people can reduce mistakes, complaints and abortive work which can be significant overheads for public services. With much more accountability, these can be a big risk to reputations. As well as helping maintain or restore the credibility of public services, involvement can also improve political engagement. It can create a sense of ownership and control that, arguably, produces better outcomes.'

*One Nation*, the Labour Party's policy review published in October 2014,[1] argued that there is now a political imperative to explore these ideas: 'as in the age of steam and the age of railways, our new digital age is radically changing society. Technology is facilitating new cultural practises and new models of production. The new economy uses teamwork and it creates relationships with consumers to co-invent new products, ideas and cultural meaning. Central government, big bureaucracies and corporations, faced with complexity and unpredictability, are all losing the power they once had to shape the world in their image. Their hierarchies and bureaucratic structures cannot keep up.'

However, as Gill pointed out, it is still early days for co-production as a realistic alternative: 'There is little shared research and few tried and tested models of co-design and co-production in Britain. There's therefore little guidance on what works well in what circumstances, and what is needed to support co-design or co-production processes within or between particular communities or across different services.'

Gill suggests that the next mayor should establish a Co-Production Academy to give Londoners the skills, confidence and opportunity to design and run the services that matter to them. It would bring together practitioners, policy makers, purchasers and providers to identify opportunities, support the spread of good practise and measure impact. On the blog she outlined the brief in more detail than we have space for here and concludes: 'In a time of diminishing alternatives, this is a real opportunity to creatively co-operate at the scale that is needed.'

## Six Knotty Questions

These approaches aren't especially radical but they would be unusual, not least because there is currently a path dependency in the commissioning of public services which ensures that the outcome lies within the limited vision and experience of the commissioner. They specify the service that they expect, often in great detail, rather than the problem that they need to resolve. It is not realistic to expect different outcomes unless and until the process is changed.

Barcelona has shown the way with six 'challenges' and a call for 'high-impact solutions'.[92] Social isolation is one of the challenges and anyone is welcome to bid. Reducing bike theft (rather than installing a network of lockable bike racks) is another Barcelona challenge that we might recognise in London. Transforming the commissioning process in this way opens up the possibility of new and potentially far better provision, and of entirely different delivery partners.

Perhaps the next London mayor could publish a similar set of six knotty questions. Reducing social isolation should certainly feature on our list as well as Barcelona's. Pioneering the process would establish helpful precedents for other public service providers in London as well as, potentially, transformational responses to six wicked issues.

## Make the Weather

Some mayoral aspirants may feel that vocal support for public services that are avowedly local, governed by the community and planned and delivered in partnership with service users is quite stretching enough, but this could be just a beginning. Suppose the next London mayor went further and began to explore specific targets for the continuing evolution of coproduced neighbourhood services. How might that look? Here's one example.

Research shows that almost everybody would prefer to die at home but, unless things change, almost all of us will die in hospital.[93] Quite apart from the importance of public opinion and the case for compassion, there are good economic arguments and, as the proportion of older people grows year on year, even more political ones for developing a broad and purposeful city-wide strategy for end-of-life care, taking it out of unfamiliar institutions and into the places we love. What about a neighbourhood-based co-production service for end of life care? How might that look?

Of course, the mayor's operational responsibilities in this area amount to next to nothing but their soft power should not be underestimated. In 2008, new mayor Boris Johnson made clear his dissatisfaction with the Metropolitan Police Commissioner Sir Ian Blair. The rules are clear: commissioners are hired and fired by the Home Secretary. She and even the prime minister were reported to be supporting a commissioner who seemed confident of weathering the storm but within days of the whispers beginning, Sir Ian was packing away his truncheon. When the London mayor chooses to flex his or her mandate almost everyone must listen.

Throughout the world, the big change-making mayors are advocates and torch bearers. The vast majority of London's 8.5 million citizens would prefer to die at home. That's quite an army.

In *The Metropolitan Revolution* Bruce Katz and Jennifer Bradley argued that cities are networks, not governments.[7] This is even more true in London than it is in other parts of the world where mayors have more formal powers. A transformative vision here can only take flight with the active engagement of many partners. Such engagement, and the structures that support it, must be built from an understanding not just of what works but also of why it works.

London government does not need new layers of bureaucracy but a small number of focused institutions, drawing on the strengths and assets of the city and developing them further could be important planks of a progressive mayoral programme. The Co-Production Academy is exactly the kind of relatively low-investment institution building that could best exploit the superpowers and in time release a wave of change across the capital influenced, perhaps inspired, by the mayor but neither owned nor directed by their office.

These are ambitious ideas but, as Louise concluded, 'We know how to improve the lives of individuals and communities. The good news is that it doesn't take any more resources to do it but it does take courageous public sector leaders who are willing to follow evidence and abandon the rhetoric of standardisation and scale.'

Might the next London mayor be that leader? He or she won't make all the rules, and they won't be directly responsible for commissioning very much at all, but they could change the weather.

## Under One Roof

We noted earlier how the design and use of the built environment can bring people together, leading naturally to the evolution of a peer network. The location of public services under one roof could be similarly beneficial. We may not need the dentist very often, or the GP or the social worker, and we may rarely visit the library or the Housing Office or the police station, but we would get to know the staff and our neighbours far better if these services operated from one neighbourhood building serving everyone. Strong supportive communities grow on common ground in places we share.

The public estate is a huge national resource with a book value of £354 billion.[94] Promoting the collaborative management of that estate and, in particular, the principle of Under One Roof – public agencies operating from shared neighbourhood buildings – would help in the delivery of joined-up services and in the development of local networks. The colocation of universal and specialist services also helps with overcoming some of the perceived stigma that might otherwise reduce the take up of some services; it would improve the quality of the provision and it would drive efficiencies, saving money on building costs and on front- and back-office functions. This might even allow for investment in improvements – maybe a café or a play area in the waiting space instead of the serried ranks of fixed plastic seating.

Ultimately, and with appropriate safeguards, the neighbourhood estate might be given over to endow a local community trust. The financial asset would give substance to the rhetoric of local ownership and common wealth. Perhaps it could pay for the Right to Space or the 1000 Flowers strategy, or it could even be used as a cornerstone for investing in the realisation of other local aspirations – a new and communal version of a property-owning democracy.

Some local authorities are already rationalising, but coordination with other public sector asset holders is, at best, patchy. The next London mayor might compile a London Register of Public Assets – a kind of twenty-first century Domesday Book, cataloguing the public estate in the capital – and then argue for the collaborative approach. There are precedents and models. The LGA, for example, have been developing the idea of using special-purpose vehicles to lead on the delivery of such plans with a view to optimising the value of the assets.[94] It's good stewardship, smart management and thoughtful leadership.

A rambling, disjointed and often dilapidated public estate is the face that local, regional and national government currently presents to most of its citizens in the capital. Driving the colocation of public services in the neighbourhoods of London is a bricks-and-mortar proposal with immediate practical benefits but it would also have a wider totemic purpose. It would say that in this great city everybody matters. Here, in our neighbourhood, are good-quality services run by thoughtful people with respect for you, for the limitations on the public purse and for the convenience and the contribution of the people in our community.

## (4) Champion the Willing Citizen: Recognise, Motivate and Inspire Replication
### Time-Based Currency

Co-design, garage sales and plotting sheds, and everything else we have suggested here, are dependant on our willing engagement. If that makes these suggestions sound naive, reflect for a moment on the success of the National Blood Service. At first blush it seems improbable, even counterintuitive, that so many people would willingly endure the inconvenience of donating precious fluids to a stranger without recompense. It is the ultimate gift without hope of reciprocation. In fact, more than 2 million donations are collected every year, and the NHS depends on them.[95] The service has become an institution, part of our culture, and a process in which thousands of us engage willingly and regularly.

Such results could not be bought – we give but we would not sell – but this does not mean that the contribution should be taken for granted. Too often in a big city we feel overlooked and unimportant. We want to be wanted. Recognition in this context isn't about conventional financial remuneration or even rights and responsibilities

– both are too base and transactional. It is about the simple reciprocities, the give and take, of a place where people matter.

Becky Booth built on her experience with Spice, running a time-based currency, to suggest that the next London mayor should support something similar for London: 'a currency that values everyone's time equally… For each hour you give, you earn a paper or online time credit; these credits can then be spent on the large number of cultural, leisure and learning opportunities that London has to offer.'[96] Effectively a gift, from one neighbour to another.

In the twenty-four communities where Spice already run the scheme, more than half of the people involved had never volunteered or had not volunteered regularly before time credits were introduced, and more than 70 per cent say they now feel more confident, more valued and more connected to others in their community. Becky pointed out that 'this currency also provides a meaningful way for the business community to give back to London. The ways of spending credits are as diverse as the interests of the participants. You can visit the Tower of London, watch a film, take a course at City Lit, swim at Parliament Hill Lido, get a lift to a doctors appointment, go to the theatre.'

A time-based currency is a mechanism for recognising and rewarding the gift of time. It is a way of saying thank you and, the evidence suggests, it leads to more volunteering. We don't want payment but we do like to be appreciated.

## A Big Story about a Mayor of Small Things

Barely does a day go by when Londoners don't hear on the radio or read in the evening paper about the latest views or activities of the London mayor. Eight and a half million people give the London mayor a big platform and a mighty megaphone. It is this capacity to speak, and be heard, that can turn a set of worthy initiatives into a coherent strategy and make it more than the sum of its parts. The next London mayor must curate a new narrative, showcase ideas in action and inspire with their enthusiasm for a vision of what London might become. In short, they must tell the stories. Sometimes with words, sometimes pictures and sometimes something completely different. Bogotá's former mayor Antanas Mockus, for instance, focused attention on traffic fatalities with mime artists at street corners, and as part of his quest to improve neighbourly relations issued 350,000 'thumbs up' or 'thumbs down' cards for citizens to approve or disapprove of one another's' behaviour.[97]

Novelist Ben Okri says we become the stories that we tell ourselves, they are our 'secret reservoir of values... Change the stories that individual and nations live by and tell themselves and we change the individuals and the nations.'[98] The next London mayor should use their platform to tell the stories about a city where communities thrive and everybody matters, about the 'simple reciprocities', the 'neighbourhood acupuncture' and the little things that matter most.

Of course there is an argument that a bigger story, less ordinary, would be a far more effective way of changing London, but actually the science of influence tells us otherwise. The work of psychologists Leif Nelson and Michael Norton is a good example.[99]

In their experiments they asked sample groups of people to list ten features of a superhero or ten features of Superman. When then asked to volunteer for community service the people in the superhero group were twice as likely to sign up and, three months later, four times more likely to show up than the Superman group.

Why did that happen? Because in considering the general attributes of a superhero we think about characteristics we can relate to. Reflecting on these attainable attributes shapes our behaviour. Superman's powers, in contrast, feel unattainable. Reflecting on those attributes does not affect our behaviour.

That's why we don't have to wait for another London Olympics to inspire a generation, and, in fact, it would be better if we didn't. The London Olympics were wonderful in many ways but very few of us can realistically aspire to athletic superstardom, so watching the supermen and superwomen did not change our day-to-day behaviour. If and when there is a next time, very few of us expect to win the 100 metres but don't we all intend to sign up as one of the purple-shirted volunteers that we so envied and admired?

A Gallery of Greater Londoners – 'Ordinary people making life better' – featured in posters on buses and stations and trains and changed every week is, the science demonstrates, far more likely to influence what we do than showcasing the unattainable. Not a handful of heroes but a city full of greater Londoners.

London has not lacked in recent years for a mayor who could tell a good story, but next time it needs to be the right one – inclusive and visionary, stretching but attainable, healing and honest and just. Narrative and activity reinforcing one another. A theory of change driven first by the parts and then by the alchemy. A big story about a mayor of small things.

## (5) Learn to Improve: Measure and Evaluate Social Indicators

### A London Index

The duty to measure and to evaluate, to be held to account and to learn to improve is a responsibility that must run through all the ideas in this book and particularly through those in this chapter. There will be reservations about the investment of time and money in community building and, as Nick Stanhope has pointed out, it would be easy but wrong to be vague:

> The concept of social capital is complex and varied, but that doesn't mean that we have to be vague and fluffy about it. Huge progress has been made in how social capital is traced and measured, with the ONS Social Capital Question Bank as a good example. London's mayor should draw on all this progress, add to it and take the lead in rigorous longitudinal studies, randomised control tests and peer reviews.

Academics have shown that you can make meaningful measurement of a seemingly intangible idea. Professor Robert Sampson has tracked thousands of Chicago residents over many years, gathering data on everything from local fundraising and the return of lost letters to levels of blood donation and the proportion of heart attack victims who received CPR from bystanders.[31] He and his team identified a quality they have called 'collective efficacy' – local residents' propensity to intervene on behalf of one another. Communities with higher rates of collective efficacy suffered lower rates of crime, teenage pregnancy and social disorder, even after taking account of the impact of poverty and of family ties.

This kind of evidence, and evidence gathering, will be very important around new programmes which might seem like a 'nice to have' but peripheral to the big issues. As we suggested at the start of this chapter and as Professor Sampson, and others, have shown, nothing could be further from the truth, but that needs to be proved here in London.

Michael Green proposed the application of a London-wide Social Progress Index[100] – the new and, as yet, only comprehensive international measure of a nation's performance registered solely in terms of social and environmental indicators. John Page suggested that our many universities might be encouraged to think of themselves as a community resource,[101] 'inviting communities into the academy, organising research projects that have practical impact for the communities concerned and staging seminars in the community that are relevant to the community.'

Combining the two ideas: a London index that was codesigned and coproduced with and by the citizens of London and its learning institutions, that established the social indicators most relevant to Londoners and that measured our city's progress against those indices would help London citizens and the next mayor to understand what works best and how to do it better.

San Francisco's 'Government barometer' updates residents every quarter on progress across a whole range of measures, from public health to police performance to bin collection and voting registration.[102] And New York's plaNYC is a twenty-year vision for the city's sustainability that the New York City Office for Long Term Planning and Sustainability leads and reports on.[103]

This work in other cities shows that measuring the success of community building is not only possible but vital, and that the boldest city leaders do it collaboratively and openly. Measures that have value if imposed from outside are even more powerful if developed and agreed amongst residents, prioritising the issues that they feel are most important. The health of our neighbourhoods, no less than the efficiency of our transport system, can be measured, and it should be.

Robert Kennedy once observed that the American GNP 'measures everything except that which makes life worthwhile and tells us everything about America except why we are proud that we are Americans.'[104] We need the opposite from the next London mayor: a robust measurement process reflecting what matters to us and driving the outcomes that will make us proud to be Londoners.

## LAST WORDS: A CITY WHERE EVERYBODY MATTERS

When Linda Woolston argued on Changing London in November 2013[105] that Sunderland is friendlier than London and asked 'why can't London be more like Sunderland?' the piece could have been easily dismissed. It didn't look like serious politics.

That reaction would have been a big mistake. Linda struck a nerve. Her blog was more widely read, liked, tweeted and shared than almost any other.

'My call to a future London mayor', wrote Linda, 'is to enable London to be the most connected capital ... to factor in the opportunity to create human connection rather than eliminate it ... to make London special for its people and community as well as all the other wonderful things it has to offer.'

Others developed a similar theme: 'we desperately need a mayor with the courage and imagination to raise up our collective sense of possibility, to generate the hopefulness necessary to transform London into the world's foremost city of cooperation' wrote Steve Wyler.

'The infrastructural stuff, running the tube and bus network, looking after the main roads, seems easy by comparison', said Richard McKeever, 'but managing the countless small neighbourhoods in their kaleidoscope patterns is the key to making a positive difference to the lives of ordinary Londoners.'

And, contrary to first impressions, the politics could hardly be more serious. Andy Thornton[106] pointed out that 'people who don't sense that they own the area in which they have full democratic rights and responsibilities will lose sight of the point of democracy.' Thirty-eight per cent voter turnout in the 2012 mayoral election? Less than 20 per cent in two wards? Julian Dobson's Plotting Sheds were a neat pun but addressed a critical issue. Others quoted Eleanor Roosevelt: 'Where, after all, do universal human rights begin? In small places, close to home. Unless these rights have meaning there, they have little meaning anywhere.'[107]

'Do we want a London mayor', ended Wyler, 'who will seek to win status and popularity with grandiose projects and thereby perpetuate power and control in the hands of the few or do we want a mayor who sees the goal as lifting London up from its foundations, investing in its neighbourhoods, building cooperative communities and thereby releasing the vast resources and resourcefulness of London's most precious commodity, its people?'

We think that question should be put to the voters by a mayoral candidate who offers Londoners a serious alternative at the next election – a city where neighbourhoods thrive and everybody matters.

# 4

# A Fair City

## The Tough Stuff

London is home to some of the world's biggest businesses and its richest people. It is the world's preeminent financial centre, contributes over a fifth of the UK's GDP and produces more than Switzerland.[108]

Yet a third of our children grow up in poverty.[23] This is a disgrace to our city, incompatible with any claim to civic success, and the message from contributors to Changing London has been very clear: the next mayor must tackle it hard.

It is not enough to talk solely about the poorest: this is a problem for us all. The richest Londoners can live up to twenty-five years longer than those on the lowest incomes.[6] Our highest-paid executives earned more in the first two working days of 2015 than the average Briton will earn over the entire 365,[109] and the average house price increased by twice the average wage last year.[110]

London's next mayor should be clear: a growing gap between rich and poor – increasingly between the rich and the rest – is not merely the unfortunate byproduct of progress in London; it is the antithesis. And strong 'growth' is nothing more than a pyrrhic victory if it comes at the expense of the livelihoods of people here or elsewhere, or if the benefits accrue only to a tiny minority. We need a new narrative of fair growth. Not fairness *or* growth but both.

The previous two chapters have taken on vital issues that might nonetheless be seen as uncontroversial; making London a better place to grow up, and strengthening the communities in which we live. This chapter focuses instead on what Jon Miller and Lucy Parker called the 'angriest fault-lines' of society, the tough stuff; our next mayor must have the courage to take them on.

Despite the living wage achieving near consensual political approval and an increasing profile, low pay in London is moving in the opposite direction: 18 per cent of jobs are now low paid, up from 13 per cent in 2011.[111] Unaffordable housing now tops the list of issues facing Londoners according to polls, closely followed by low wages.[112] The children we spoke to at the Discover Children's Story Centre were clear: 'People should not be poor in London. Everyone should have enough for the basics – food, housing, clothes.'

But R. H. Tawney observed that what rich people call the problem of the poor, poor people call the problem of the rich.[113] We clearly need a more thoughtful approach at the bottom, but poverty is as much about inequality as it is about absolutes, and the differentials have exploded in London in recent years. We also need a more thoughtful approach at the top.

At the moment there is something very close to a received wisdom in the prevailing political, economic and commercial orthodoxies that holds that a determined assault on the worst excesses of inequality at home and abroad could not be undertaken without absenting the UK from important world markets, wrecking our national economy and rendering any politicians who argue otherwise officially unelectable for the rest of their natural lives. This, we think, is balderdash. Is it really necessary for Britain to be the only country in the G7 group of leading economies where inequality has increased during this century?[114] Challenges to the orthodoxy are frequently dismissed as naive or, worse, 'ideological', but the status quo is itself deeply rooted in the same. The next London mayor must challenge the poisonous fiction that a prosperous society is necessarily an unequal one.

We can take heart from New York, where Bill de Blasio won the mayoral election in 2013 by telling the tale of a widening gap in income and opportunity between rich and poor. He argued that a growing city can only claim success if the proceeds are fairly shared, and

New York's voters overwhelmingly agreed.[115] Three-quarters of Londoners say they would also support government action to reduce the gap between high and low earners.[116]

A study into 'cities of opportunity' for business ranked London at the top by a healthy margin, but a closer look reveals that our city scores well on all the things that don't much matter to most citizens – 'technology readiness', 'economic clout' and 'city gateway' – and performs very badly on those indicators that actually affect the quality of life of most Londoners – cost of living or transport, access to green space.[20] It corroborates the results of another 'good growth' index – compiled by the same private sector consultant – which looks at transport, work–life balance, inequality, health and income, in which London ranked near the bottom.[117] How can London simultaneously be a good place for business but a bad place for most of the people who work in those same businesses, and for everyone else too? This separation of the interests of 'business' from the interests of individuals, families and communities is artificial and distracting – a good mayor would bridge the divide.

## Telling a New Story

The mayor doesn't have executive power over the most obvious routes to tackling inequality – tax rates, wages, social security. But, as we have argued, the mayor enjoys a voice, a visibility and a capacity to convene that is unparalleled in British politics.

On this agenda the mayor should be an activist and a convener, a campaigner and an advocate, a thinker and at all times a leader, telling a new story about our city.

They should say to our poorest citizens, poverty is not your fault but we must work together to tackle it. Know that London is unashamedly on your side.

They should say to our wealthiest citizens, we are all citizens of London and share our streets, our services and our communities. We ask not that you give more – although charity is important – but that you take less in the first place. Strong communities are built on the principle of fairness not patronage, however generous.

They should say to our businesses, thriving businesses are vital for the success of our city; we respect the importance of the executive pay packet, the share options scheme and the size of your balance sheet but we do not revere them. We value businesses that employ their staff well, pay taxes willingly, look after the environment diligently and fairly distribute their profits.

They should say to all London's citizens, we do not judge success by the size of our financial district or the 'competitiveness' of our corporate tax regime but by the power we all wield, the opportunities we all enjoy and the wealth we all share.

These issues cannot be tackled in the first hundred days, with a few set-piece speeches and a couple of policy announcements. They will rely on a mayor who looks to the future, and thinks deeply and seriously about the nature of the society and the city we want to live in. A mayor who turns a quick-win, soundbite culture of political leadership into sustained stewardship of our city and its economy.

We hold out hope that a mayor of sufficient calibre could bring all Londoners with them on the journey, but we recognise that this may not always be possible. The former mayor of Bogotá Enrique Penelosa said: 'If you want to really construct equality and not just talk about it, if you really want change, there has to be conflict. Some people are benefited by the status quo, and if you want to change the status quo people will complain.' The next London mayor should not pick fights unnecessarily but nor should they shirk from their responsibility where conflict is unavoidable.

How would London look if re-engineered around the interests of all Londoners? We suggest four guiding principles, around which this chapter is based:
   (1) On poverty: having enough to live on should be an entitlement in a rich city, not a privilege
   (2) On wealth: remuneration distorted beyond the dreams of avarice is no more useful here and no more welcome than abject poverty.
   (3) On business: businesses of good character are defined not by shareholder return or contribution to GDP, but by the difference they make to the lives of Londoners.

(4) On housing: houses in London are for people to live in and there must be enough for everyone. They should no longer be treated as investment vehicles.

# (1) On Poverty: Having Enough to Live on Should Be an Entitlement in a Rich City, Not a Privilege

Despite the riches on our doorstep, London is home to some of the UK's poorest neighbourhoods. A staggering one-quarter of adults and one-third of children live in poverty.[118] Almost 96,000 Londoners visited food banks in the last year.[119]

The recession hit poor Londoners particularly hard – the incomes of the poorest plunged by 24 per cent[120] – but the pattern had been established already. Low, stagnant wages and a rapidly rising cost of living have left people struggling to get by.

## A London Minimum Wage and a Fair Pay Commission

The introduction of the minimum wage was a powerful statement but, as Kitty Ussher explained,[121] it has had a much smaller impact in London than elsewhere in the country, because wages here were slightly higher to begin with. Kitty argued for a new London minimum wage, set higher than the national rate to reflect the fact that London's economy is different from that of the rest of the country and the cost of living so much higher. A rise of 44p here would mean it was economically equivalent to that for the rest of the country. Ultimately, she estimates that the London rate could be 20 per cent higher than the national rate with very little impact on jobs. She argues that the Low Pay Commission – who recommend the rate each year – should put forward a separate London rating.

To add to the pressure, the mayor should establish a London Fair Pay Commission to publish its own estimate of a viable London minimum wage each year, with the aim of assuming the equivalent role to the Low Pay Commission once the change is instituted. The London Fair Pay Commission could also take on the GLA's role in calculating the London living wage, and perhaps extend its remit to top pay as well.

There is evidence for the effectiveness of region- or city-specific minimum wage rates from the US, where cities and states have the power to raise their minimum wage higher than the federally mandated minimum and have done so successfully for years, to reflect the local economy.[122] As inequality becomes a big political issue some areas are seizing the initiative: Seattle recently voted through an enormous rise from $9.10 to $15 per hour, and thirty-four state legislatures are now considering raising their minimum wages.[123]

The mayor doesn't have the power to set the minimum wage but should make the case to government on our behalf.

## Enforce the Minimum Wage

Meanwhile, Andy Hull[124] pointed out that many workers in London don't even get paid the minimum wage, because enforcement – the responsibility of national government – is woefully inadequate. The Low Pay Commission found that, in eight London boroughs, one in twenty workers is paid less than the minimum wage, and a Newham Council study found that a shocking one in five reported earning less than the statutory minimum.[125] Andy and others argue that responsibility for enforcement should be devolved to local authorities, who are much better placed than national government to police compliance. The GLA's economy committee has suggested piloting it initially in boroughs that are keen to take on the responsibility.[126] The mayor should press home the idea with HMRC.

## The Living Wage

The living wage has won the enthusiastic support of both mayors, has more than 800 organisations signed up across the country, and has benefited thousands of workers to the tune of hundreds of millions of pounds since its launch by London citizens in 2001. The current mayor has said he wants it to be the norm in London by 2020, and the public sector has led the way, with TfL, the Metropolitan Police and the GLA all living-wage employers.[127]

It's a powerful movement and an impressive story, but take a step back and the picture is far less rosy. In fact, just as the living wage has grown in reputation, the number of people being paid less than the living wage has grown too. Rapidly: by 45,000 in 2013 alone. Last year 18 per cent of Londoners were paid less than the living wage, up from only 12 per cent in 2009.[111]

It reflects a trend across the UK, where rising prices and stagnant earnings are pushing more and more people below the low-pay threshold. The London Assembly's Economy Committee said it was 'concerned that the mayor's plans for normalising the living wage in London fail to take account of the scale of the challenge. The current rate of progress is insufficient to achieve the mayor's objective.'[127]

While many of the most high-profile signatories to the campaign have been city firms like KPMG and Barclays, the real problems lie with industries that have so far failed to engage: retail, hospitality, catering, cleaning and social care.[127] Jobs in retail, hotels and restaurants accounted for half of all low-paid work in London, while the high proportion of low-paid jobs in social care should be a source of particular shame to the public sector, from where most social care is funded.

Some local authorities have extended the campaign to the companies they contract from. Glasgow's Labour leader Gordon Matheson, for instance, announced in November 2014 that 'Glasgow City Council's procurement policy will be changed to give a material advantage to employers who pay the living wage ... further reward those companies that demonstrate that they offer real community benefits, that don't employ staff on exploitative zero hours contracts, and that don't have a track record of blacklisting trade union members.'[128]

We should keep a close eye on Bill de Blasio in New York, who entered office promising to take on big companies who take advantage of the city's welfare system. He called them 'corporate welfare queens' and argued: 'If we're subsidizing companies, we have every right to demand a living wage for the people they pay.'[129]

To his credit, Mayor Johnson has thrown his considerable rhetorical weight behind the living-wage campaign, but his successor must go further. This battle will be won company by company, one workplace at a time, and requires a mayor willing to put in the hard grind, working with London Citizens and others who have led the campaign from the start. In particular, those sectors that dominate low-paid work but have so far refused to engage must be dragged or coaxed to the table however possible. Some easy targets might include the government departments who have so far refused to sign up.

The living wage should form a crucial part of the Mayor's Pledge (see below) and must be on the tip of the mayor's tongue every time a business leader passes within earshot. The People's Share (also see below) will give the mayor an opportunity to pursue it at AGMs under the gaze of the media and the public.

## Stronger Unions

A hotel cleaner in Manhattan earns three times more than their counterpart working for the same chain in London, even though New York's minimum wage is considerably lower. The reason: 70 per cent of Manhattan's cleaners belong to a union, compared with between 2 and 4 per cent in London.[130] Stronger unions are a surer and more efficient route to higher pay than minimum wages or even living wages, because negotiations can respond to specific sectors and prevailing economic conditions in a way that a blunt nationwide floor can never do. Evidence suggests that unions are good for productivity and lead to lower levels of executive pay.[131] Very few mainstream politicians will be caught making a strong case for unions these days – the London mayor could start a new trend, urging Londoners to join a union and employers to work with them, and pledging to engage constructively themselves in negotiations where necessary. They should make the case that it is the responsibility of a good employer to ensure their staff have the opportunity to join a union.

## A Strategy for Tackling Youth Unemployment

Young Londoners have been particularly badly hit by the recession: youth unemployment now stands at 25 per cent, and a constant influx of young skilled people from around the country leaves unskilled young people, in particular, struggling to find jobs. The Work Foundation argued that despite plenty of initiatives, 'London lacks a strategic vision for tackling youth unemployment.'[132] The mayor could lead Londoners, particularly young people, in developing one.

On Changing London Andrew Attfield[133] offered the example of Barts NHS Trust in east London, which offers apprenticeships to local residents and provides supported routes into entry-level jobs. They know that jobs and higher wages improve health, ultimately reducing demand for their services.

We could learn from Chicago, where the Mayor's Plan for Economic Growth and Jobs ensured its colleges were properly preparing students for jobs in the city's most successful and up-and-coming business sectors, with businesses helping design curricula and providing internships and apprenticeships.[134]

Bharat Mehta[135] explained the advantages of investing in skills: 'Low paid workers receiving training on the job see their pay increase by 13 per cent on average – two thirds higher than those that don't. Unlocking the £2 billion Adult Skills Budget – with eligibility for full funding for Level 2 training extended to those in work and identified as most at risk of low pay and poor progression, could help. Currently this funding cannot be spent on supporting low paid workers.' The mayor could pressure BIS to implement this relatively simple measure. Better still, perhaps, they should argue for devolution of the budgets for training and skills in London from BIS to the GLA. This is exactly the sort of programme that needs to reflect local needs and opportunities and is best administered close to the ground. It's a power they should press for.

## Encourage Benefit Take-Up

Finally, social security is a vital source of income for Londoners, both in and out of work. The mayor has very little influence over one of the most centralised social security systems in the world but must at least speak out against the benefit cap, which is driving families out of London and away from communities; a higher rate in London should reflect the higher costs of living here. He or she could also use their platform to try and tell a different story about our embattled social security system, recognising the value it brings to London and harrying government for, in particular, the devolution of housing benefit and employment support (as suggested by the London Finance Commission[136]), and in time for other aspects too.

The mayor could also lead a benefits take-up campaign in London. In Miami, city officials realised how many of their residents were entitled to but not claiming one of the US's key benefits: the earned income tax credit, similar to the working tax credit in the UK. The mayor, Manny Diaz, called on churches across the city to help raise awareness of the payment amongst their parishioners. The next year, earned income tax credit payments to Miami residents rose by $42 million. The mayor's chief of staff said it 'could be considered one of the largest investments in our city in a one-year period'. Social security is generally spent quickly and in the local economy – the best kind of regeneration money.[137]

In the UK billions of pounds in benefits go unclaimed every year. To take just one example, pensioner poverty in the UK would almost halve (from 15 per cent to 9 per cent) if older people took up all the means-tested benefits they were entitled to.[138] Imagine what a concerted effort amongst Londoners, led by the mayor but relying on every part of civil society, could achieve in reducing poverty in our later years.

## (2) On Wealth: Remuneration Distorted Beyond the Dreams of Avarice Is No More Useful Here and No More Welcome than Abject Poverty

Two days into the working year senior executives in the UK's biggest businesses have earned more than the average worker will take home in the entire year.[109] As Deborah Hargreaves explained,[139] it would take someone on average earnings more than 600 years to earn the £17 million received by the highest-paid chief executive of a British company in 2013: Angela Ahrendts at Burberry. The recession tore an already divided city even further apart; while the richest saw their wealth increase dramatically, the poorest found their income plunging by 24 per cent.[120]

Whilst Labour's shadow business secretary Chuka Umunna may say that he doesn't 'have a problem with people making lots of money',[140] 77 per cent of Londoners feel that the city is becoming a place for the super rich while people on normal incomes are squeezed out.[21]

This is not a phenomenon unique to London but it is at its most extreme here.[141] Between 2000 (when the data was first collected) and 2013 the pay gap between the top 10 per cent and the bottom 10 per cent of earners in London rose by 14 per cent, compared with 5 per cent nationally.[142] Executive pay has quadrupled in the past ten years while workforce wages are, in real terms, back at the same level as in 2003. More of the super rich call London home than any other city on earth.[143] If the minimum wage had kept pace with FTSE 100 executive pay since it was introduced, it would now be almost £19 an hour.[144]

There is a widely held assumption that this extreme and widening inequality of income and wealth is a sign of the success of London's economy and should be tolerated, at the very least, if not indulged. Our current mayor put this more clearly than most when he said: 'it would be wrong to persecute the rich, and madness to try and stifle wealth creation, and futile to try to stamp out inequality'. Instead, he said we should 'help those who genuinely cannot compete; and ... provide opportunity for those who can'.[145]

Extremely high income is acceptable, this argument goes, because the rich give to charity and pay their taxes, fulfilling their social responsibility in cash. Johnson again: 'I wish the snob value and prestige that the Americans attach to acts of giving would somehow manifest itself here, or manifest itself more vividly'.

Giving to charity is a fine and righteous deed, but few things are more troubling than that fashionable explanation: 'I want to give something back.' It may be unworthy but we long to reply: 'it may not be so necessary if you hadn't taken such a lot in the first place.'

Philanthropy is undemocratic: it affords power to those with enough money to give some away. The leveraging of tax is at least democratically determined, but the richest are also most adept at avoiding it. Even so, the highest-earning 1 per cent pay almost 30 per cent of income tax, which some use to justify inequality (Boris Johnson said 'we should fête them and decorate them and inaugurate a new class of tax hero'). In reality all it reflects is the gross inequality of income that means so few earn so much. Consider the extreme in which one person earns everything; he (it would likely be a he) would pay all the income tax in what would be a grossly unfair society.

Why does it matter? Sean Baine[146] explained: 'We know, from the book *The Spirit Level* by Professors Wilkinson and Pickett, that more unequal societies are bad for almost everyone – the well off as much as the poor. Almost every social problem – ill-health, low levels of trust, violence, mental illness, drug abuse – is more likely to occur in a less equal society... If inequality in London could be reduced to Nordic and Japanese levels then obesity could be halved, mental illness cut by two thirds, teenage births by nearly three quarters. Trust levels would nearly double.'[147]

Peter Baker[148] explained why it is so important for all our health: 'equal societies make a whole series of better collective decisions. Being healthy requires collective decisions on provision of healthcare, on acceptable levels of air pollution, on provision of green parks and good cycle lanes.'

This is both a practical and a moral case for greater equality because the two are intertwined. Perhaps Aristotle was exaggerating when he said there is no friendship among the unequal,[149] but the extremes of separation inevitably exact a price on personal relationships and shape the city that we share. How can those on an average wage relate easily to those who live in very different neighbourhoods when they are in London, often spending much of their leisure time in other homes, and who don't use the same schools, the same public transport, the same health service?

Sky-high salaries and extreme wealth damage our health, detract from our well-being and tear our city apart. And they are not – as some would have us believe – a necessary part of a functioning economy. Other thriving economies across Europe succeed without the extremes of inequality that scar London. As Deborah pointed out: 'In 1979, a company director or top banker was on a package that amounted to 14–15 times the average wage for the workforce at our biggest companies. That multiple is now 133 times.'

Even New York – probably London's closest equivalent city across the world – has resolved to tackle inequality. Bill de Blasio, recently elected mayor on a pledge to bring the 'two New Yorks' back together, has said: 'There are some who have taken issue with our commitment to this cause – who say that income inequality is just a fact of life, and that attempts to remedy it are simply sowing the seeds of class warfare. But we know better. We understand that allowing the income gap to stretch further isn't simply a threat to those at the bottom – but to every New Yorker.'[150]

## Controlling High Pay

Three measures in particular would help to bring down excessive pay.

Greater transparency of current pay levels within companies would shine a light on the disparities between employees and their senior management, as is now required of US companies by the Dodd–Frank Act. The public sector in London has a reasonably good record on this, with bodies including the GLA, TfL and the Metropolitan Police publishing their pay ratios. The TfL Commissioner earns £348,444 per year for managing a £9 billion organisation[151] (in contrast, the aforementioned Burberry Chief Executive earned £17 million for leading a company with a turnover for 2013 of £2.3 billion[152]).

Installing employees on company boards would anchor remuneration decisions in the realities of pay for the majority of the workforce. The High Pay Centre have outlined how companies should offer elected representatives of the workforce a place on the board and the remuneration committee, accompanied by training for employee directors. They point out that the UK is ranked 26 out of 27 EU countries for the level of worker participation in company decision making, and point to countries like Germany and Sweden where this is the norm.[153]

Introducing a maximum ratio between the pay of the median or lowest-paid worker and the highest paid would also help. The latter could be instituted voluntarily by the firm (as John Lewis have famously done, along with new bank TSB on their split from Lloyds) or could be incentivised or even imposed by government. In a report for the current government, economist Will Hutton recommended a 20:1 pay ratio for the public sector,[154] which we and others argue should be extended to private sector contractors as well. John Lewis and TSB have adopted a less ambitious 75:1 ratio.[153] Establishing the principle of a ratio, even at this high level, will be an important first step, which is why we suggest it as a starting point. The London Fair Pay Commission could track and advise on a suitable ratio.

Ironically, those companies that have engaged most positively with the living wage – in finance, accountancy and the city – are those with whom we actually want to be talking about wages at the top. Remuneration consultants (including the big accountancy firms) drive up pay, and remuneration committees, usually formed of city grandees and former chief executives, form a bubble of their own and should be thrown open to new membership, not least to employees.

High pay should form the second pillar of the Mayor's Pledge (see below), placed firmly alongside the living wage as two sides of the same coin – out of control pay at the top is just as damaging as poverty pay at the bottom.

## Taxation

The mayor has virtually no control over taxation in London but should certainly support the recommendations of the London Finance Commission that property and land taxes should be immediately devolved to London government.[136] Council tax in particular is deeply regressive, with the richest inhabitants of multimillion-pound houses paying only three times more than the poorest renters.[155] Extending council tax bands and revaluing London's housing stock is politically terrifying but it is essential, and can perhaps only be led by a brave, radical mayor.

## A Voluntary Tax

The London mayor cannot levy new taxes, but that hasn't stopped other city mayors from raising money from their citizens. Bogotá's former mayor Antanas Mockus asked his citizens to contribute a voluntary 10 per cent extra in tax, and an astonishing 63,000 people agreed. He is just one of several city leaders who have experimented with voluntary taxation and it is often surprisingly successful. In Maine, the councillor who introduced the Bill for a tax to fund services for older people did so after hearing pleas from residents who wanted to pay more in order to save cherished local services. Forty-one US states make it possible to donate to state-run programmes and charities via their income tax forms.[156]

A voluntary tax sounds like the ultimate oxymoron but a brave mayor could try just that in London. It could perhaps be administered with boroughs through the collection of council tax, and could harness some of what behavioural psychology has taught us about the importance of group comparison ('52 per cent of your neighbours paid a voluntary tax this year'). It should be tied to an inspiring programme that unites Londoners – perhaps a young person's jobs guarantee, a London Child Trust Fund, or a network of Play Street coordinators in every borough.

A voluntary tax doesn't address the underlying inequality of wealth and power but it is more democratic than pure philanthropy (since the elected mayor decides the goal of the programme and it is administered with what is, ultimately, public money). More importantly, it could bind Londoners together behind a shared campaign, raise some much-needed money for investment in a vital social programme, and begin to challenge the prevailing view of tax, reintroducing the idea of contribution and mutual benefit.

### A London Fairness Commission

Sean Baine made the case for a London Fairness Commission on Changing London last year,[157] arguing that 'there is no forum to consider fairness across our city, and no strategic leadership on the issue'. He proposed a London-wide commission to measure income inequality, review the evidence and develop recommendations. Not content to sit around and wait, he and My Fair London and Toynbee Hall, working with Trust for London, have fleshed out the idea and launched it. The Commission will report later this year. We urge the commissioners to be bold in their vision, and the next mayor to take its recommendations seriously.

### Get Out More

Wealth is important in part for the influence it brings. It is easy, as mayor, to meet the rich and powerful – lunch with a chief executive, dinner with a sporting star, tennis with the prime minister. If not carefully managed, access turns into unfair influence for the interests of an elite. A fair mayor would go out of their way to meet and speak with Londoners outside the usual circle. More bus drivers than business leaders, more young black men stopped by police than older white men leading the police, more children in care than council chief executives. Recently retired former mayor of Boston Tom Menino had met an astounding 57 per cent of the residents of his city during his eighteen-year tenure.[158] He described his approach: 'You have to be out there every day listening to people. When you sit in your office, you don't accomplish anything. That's part of my success. I go out there and listen.'

## (3) ON BUSINESS: WE JUDGE SUCCESS BY THE CONTRIBUTION A BUSINESS MAKES TO ALL LONDON'S CITIZENS NOT THE WEALTH IT ACCRUES FOR A MINORITY

London's businesses are vital to the success of the city and our quality of life. We judge their success by the wealth they generate and the opportunity they provide, but also the way in which this wealth and these opportunities are shared fairly between all our citizens.

The prevailing orthodoxy sees big business profitability as an end in itself, with the promise of benefits to flow down to the rest of the population. Yet even the OECD has recently rejected this trickle-down economics, finding that growth slows as inequality increases.[159] The next mayor must challenge the received wisdom. While the size of the balance sheet and the return to shareholders might be important indicators, they are not the ultimate barometer of a business's worth, because 'success' is hollow – the wrong concept entirely, in fact – if it comes at the expense of the livelihoods of people here or elsewhere, or if the benefits only accrue to a tiny minority.

A London business will only be judged of good character if alongside making profit it pays its staff at least the living wage, with its highest salaries a modest multiple of the lowest, so the highest and lowest paid can share in our city's riches; it pays tax where government intends it to and doesn't profit at the expense of people's livelihoods or the environment either here or abroad; and it provides a fair way into jobs for young people, with paid apprenticeships and advertised positions.

For many years businesses have 'given something back' to their community through old-fashioned corporate social responsibility, with a budget doled out to local charities. At its best, it is a vital support for local communities, particularly from small and local businesses. But it is not the most important contribution a business makes.

The relationship between London's biggest businesses and London government can sometimes feel unbalanced – businesses dispensing sponsorship, expertise and the occasional veiled threat, secure in their primacy, all of which London's leaders welcome with supplicant delight. We need a more respectful, more grown-up relationship on both sides, centred around the mutual recognition that we all have our different parts to play – often simultaneously – as parents, business owners, workers, shareholders and volunteers, but we are united in London by a responsibility for our city and our community and what we leave behind for our children.

This is not an anti-business screed, but it is an attempt to define business success differently. We are not interested in businesses that are profitable for their own sake but in profitable businesses of good character. This will rest on the realisation both from our mayor and those leading our biggest businesses that as people we have a shared interest in our city thriving for all its citizens; the 'success' of our corporate sector is in ultimate service of that goal.

## A People's Share

As a sign of our city's commitment to the sector, the mayor should purchase a share in each of the largest 100 businesses here. It would be a symbol of the support the city is willing to offer its businesses, but it would also highlight the expectations we have in return.

The shares would give the mayor the right to speak at the businesses' AGMs just like any other shareholder, and to make the case for a living wage, curbs on high pay, the provision of apprenticeships and honest tax contributions. It would be symbolic but powerfully so – the mayor using his or her profile and platform to stand up for business, but only business that acts in the interests of London.

Shareholder activism has achieved some impressive victories, not least in persuading one-fifth of FTSE 100 companies to adopt the living wage.[160] The mayor would bring extra publicity and pressure to bear, working closely with groups already engaged on these issues.

The People's Share is symbolic of the way in which the mayor can stand up for the interests of London and Londoners, and for London business at the same time.

## The Mayor's Pledge

At the AGM and behind the scenes the mayor would ask every business to sign up to the Mayor's Pledge. It would set out our expectations of good London employers:

- to pay at least the living wage so every London worker has enough to live on;
- to pay the highest-earning staff no more than seventy-five times the median, to publish the pay ratio, and to introduce an employee onto the board to constrain excessive pay;
- to pay the taxes government expects;
- to ensure fair opportunities for young Londoners by offering apprenticeships and paid internships.

By signing the pledge companies would show their support for the principles it contains. They would have to signal their intent to make progress on any elements they don't already comply with and, crucially, they would be required at a minimum to publish data relating to each item, including

- the proportion of their staff earning less than the living wage,
- the ratio between the highest-paid member of staff and the median salary,
- the tax paid in the UK in the previous financial year and
- details of apprenticeship schemes and internships (including the number of paid and unpaid roles).

Businesses could advertise their compliance with the pledge, and public directories of compliant businesses could be maintained by the GLA. The Mayor's Pledge could be pursued through every interaction with business – via the mayor's representation on London First and position as chair of the Local Enterprise Partnership, for example. New businesses wishing to invest in London should be invited to sign the pledge, and elements of the pledge should be built into public sector contracts and sponsorship opportunities wherever possible.

Some of these considerations – particularly around pay and opportunities for young people – apply to all employers not just profit-making businesses, and we would expect the mayor to pursue them wherever necessary, particularly through his or her influence over public sector delivery. Nonetheless, the private sector accounts for over 80 per cent of the London workforce, including the majority of the lowest and highest paid,[161] and it is there that the mayor must concentrate their efforts.

## Safety in the Crowd

On this, as with many other issues, businesses are likely to be unwilling to be the first – fearful that no one will follow and their top
talent will flee elsewhere. The mayor could help overcome this fear
by signing businesses up in principle, with the pledge only becoming active and public once a certain threshold, say fifty sign-ups, has
been reached. This approach could help overcome the timidity of our
largest companies, building momentum behind the scenes and providing some safety in numbers.

## A Financial Transactions Tax

Imagine the next mayor saying: 'Our financial services sector is a big
and a vital employer bringing wealth and opportunity. We are proud
to be world leaders and to embrace the responsibilities of leadership.
I want to start a conversation in our city. A thoughtful conversation
about the principles of a Robin Hood Tax – a tiny tax on global transactions. Hong Kong, South Africa and South Korea have found a way
to do it. Couldn't we?'

A financial transactions tax would raise vital public funds for work
here and abroad, but, just as importantly, it would help refocus the
most volatile financial markets around a longer-term, more sustainable trading model; less likely to plunge the economy back into crisis
and also, perhaps, less likely to accrue vast wealth for a tiny minority.

As Simon Chouffot[162] said, eleven European countries have already
agreed to implement it. The mayors of Brussels and Nantes have supported it. Just as wealthy interests opposed the minimum wage until
it was introduced, so opposition will surely melt away once decision
makers seize the initiative. Turkeys don't vote for Christmas, but it
might only be a matter of time and pressure. The mayor should add to
it by declaring unambiguous support for the idea.

Meanwhile, the same principle of voluntary taxation that we
touched on above could be applied to businesses too, and for that
the mechanism already exists, and is in use successfully in London:

Business Improvement Districts allow businesses in a local area to vote to levy a small extra tax on themselves, which is handed to the BID – controlled by the businesses themselves – to spend on improving the area. There are almost forty around London. Tourist-BIDs (T-BIDs) are a similar idea over a larger area, with the intention of attracting more tourists.[163] Companies could be asked to contribute to the voluntary tax alongside individuals, particularly if the money is destined to be spent on employment-related programmes for young people that will ultimately benefit business too.

## A Shorter Working Week

In the 1930s, unions (and economists including John Maynard Keynes) thought increasing mechanisation would gradually reduce the need for work, leaving more time for family, community and relaxation. After the war, the goal of reduced working hours was abandoned in favour of a focus on 'full employment' and union concentration on wages and conditions, but it's an idea that – flying in the face of consumerism and modern-day capitalism – is beginning to make a comeback.[164]

In response to the financial crisis Utah introduced a four-day work week, Gambia has a four-day public sector working week, as does the city of Gothenburg, and working hours in much of Europe are slowly declining.[164] A shorter working week brings business benefits – including higher productivity and fewer absences from work – but more importantly it would make us happier and healthier, better able to raise a family, volunteer and contribute to our communities.

The next mayor should consider a similar trial within the public sector in London, learning from Gothenburg's experience and the work of the New Economics Foundation in the UK, which has led the argument here. It would redistribute time, change what we value, and could be the spur for a revaluation of pay at all levels. Trialling it in the public sector would make a powerful case to other sectors and to the public that we value thriving lives above hours in the office.

**Holding to Account**

The financial sector dominates London's economy and yet too few of us are able to hold it to account, to understand its key institutions and underpinnings. Perhaps more rigorous public scrutiny and critique could have prevented the excesses that led to the financial crisis, and it would allow us to collectively exert a more critical oversight in future. Jamie Audsley and Emily Benn suggested embedding education about London's economy, its financial system and the ability to critique it directly into the curriculum, equipping young people with 'knowledge and skills about the reality of the city as it currently is' and the tools to change it in the future.

## (4) ON HOUSING: HOUSES IN LONDON ARE FOR PEOPLE TO LIVE IN AND THEY SHOULD NEVER BE TREATED AS INVESTMENT VEHICLES

Soaring prices for property and rentals have propelled housing up the political agenda in London; it is now Londoners' biggest concern.[165] It is not merely a symptom of inequality but a cause of it as well, as over three-quarters of new homes get snapped up by foreign investors keen to cash in.[166] High-profile and successful campaigns for access to social and affordable housing led by residents themselves – like the E15 mothers in Newham and the campaigners on the New Era Estate in Dalston – have shown the power of popular campaigning in the face of an increasingly unsustainable housing model.

Young people who want to buy their first house are priced out and forced to rent instead, at sky-high prices that make it virtually impossible to save for a deposit.[167] Increasingly, families are being forced into the private rental sector too: it now houses nearly 25 per cent of Londoners.[168] 'Affordable' housing – now defined as 80 per cent of market rent – is unaffordable for many and is in short supply, and Right to Buy has withered the council housing stock, with over half the stock in some areas bought up by private landlords.[169] An American moving to London described London as a 'parasitic city' in *The Economist* – accusing property owners of siphoning off a huge share of the city's economic gains.[170] In some developments as much as 80 per cent of new homes can be snapped up by overseas investors, and over £80 billion worth of London property is held in companies in offshore tax havens.[171]

So-called poor doors – separate entrances for social housing tenants of newly built luxury apartments – vividly illustrate the increasingly divided nature of London housing. Ostensibly to ensure that social housing tenants don't have to pay the high service charges for plush entrances and services, they have extended, particularly in the US, to include separate elevators and electrical systems, and differential (or no) access to communal facilities like play areas, gyms and pools.[172] In New York, de Blasio has promised to ban them, while in London the mayor has said he will 'discourage' their use.

However, as *London Guardian* blogger Dave Hill points out,[173] poor doors are merely a symptom of a much bigger malaise in the London housing market, which sees elected leaders reduced to squeezing concessions – like affordable housing or Section 106 payments – out of property developers cashing in on London's overheated market. Dave quotes Ken Livingstone, who candidly explained his apparent closeness to property developers while in office: 'I can get more affordable housing out of property developers than I can out of the government.'

There is no easy fix and no shortage of proposals for ways to build more good-quality houses, control the price and security of renting, retain council and social housing, and maintain a social mix and public space in the city. They take in everything from zoning laws to borrowing rules, a London Living Rent to financial devolution, use of the green belt and brownfield land, new bodies and new targets.

There is increasing consensus amongst the public and some politicians on the scale of the challenge but not on how to tackle it. Currently even the GLA and the mayor disagree on the way forward, with the GLA rejecting the mayor's housing strategy last year.[174]

On Changing London, Peter Sebastian argued[175] for a land value tax as a fairer alternative to our current council tax system, under which a £140 million penthouse in Hyde Park is liable for only £1500 in council tax each year, compared with the £50,000 a similar apartment would be liable for in New York. He also called for restrictions on foreign ownership of London homes to prevent property speculation: only people who have a National Insurance number and are paying taxes in the UK would be able to buy in central London.

Robbie de Santos argued[176] that middle-income families are being forced out of London's communities, with the richest able to buy and the poorest accessing social housing, forcing average families miles out of the city, leaving behind dangerously divided neighbourhoods. He suggests concentrating on building family-sized, shared-ownership homes, stabilising the private rental sector via long-term contracts, and making it more straightforward for middle-income people to convert and extend homes. Tim Jones[177] suggested raising public bonds to invest in buying land and building new housing, where the proceeds can be used to ensure that local residents have the skills to get the building jobs on offer and that the profits flow to local residents.

## A London Housing Challenge Panel

All of these are good ideas, but our next mayor will have to do all of them and much more if he or she is to tackle a challenge of this scale. His or her role must be first and foremost to make housing a driving priority for the city – bringing together developers, communities, central and local government, businesses and London politicians of all parties to set a radical new agenda for London's housing future, securing consensus on the scale of the problem and the plan for change.

A London Housing Challenge Panel, chaired by the mayor, could include the leaders of London Councils, charities and tenant and resident representatives, the city's major developers and estate agents, the housing minister and a treasury minister, GLA members and more. It would be set a six-month challenge to develop a bold vision over which the mayor would have final say.

Many of the solutions will have to be home grown, but we can look over the channel for some inspiration. Paris's new socialist mayor Anne Hildago has announced that the city will have first refusal on the purchase of over 8000 apartments when they come up for sale, in order to convert them to subsidised housing and maintain Paris's social mix. It sits alongside their plan to build 10,000 new apartments every year for the next six years, 70 per cent of which will be subsidised. They are working with the Paris transport authority to free up public land for building, an idea which has also been suggested for London.[178]

In Germany's three largest cities, strict new rules mean landlords cannot raise rent in the first year of a tenancy, and cannot raise rents by more than 15 per cent in three years, while landlords have to pay agents' fees rather than tenants.[179] Tenants cannot be evicted unless they don't pay their rent or the landlord wants to move back in. These rules and others have traditionally protected German cities' property markets from the kind of uncontrolled speculation that has taken hold in London, perhaps helping keep houses prices manageable as well as renting more secure.

Meanwhile, in New York, Bill de Blasio put affordable housing at the centre of his election pledge and in May 2014 unveiled a $41 billion plan for public, private, city and state funds for 200,000 affordable homes.[180] And the New York state governor – under pressure from New Yorkers, 69 per cent of whom rent their homes – is working on a tax credit for renters to ensure they benefit in the same way as homeowners will from cuts to property taxes.[181]

These ideas and those of experts from around the world could feed into the Housing Challenge process. There is no shortage of ideas; the next mayor just needs to forge a powerful, determined alliance to drive them forward.

## Last Words: An Activist Mayor

The mayor of Marinaleda, a small town near Seville, was so scandalised by the sight of people unable to feed themselves and their families that he led raids on supermarkets around his town, supervising while volunteers robbed the shops of bags of sugar, flour, pasta and oil and donated them to the local food bank. He said 'someone has to do something so that families can eat'.[182]

We are not arguing for London's next mayor to break the law but we do believe that he or she should be similarly bold in challenging the direction London's economy is taking, leading us down a new path.

We are in danger of becoming a city that unwittingly judges its success according to the interests of a tiny elite, to everyone else's cost. Being number one in the world for business is of no use to us if that doesn't translate into a higher quality of life for all Londoners. Extremes of wealth living alongside abject poverty diminish us all and are inimical to any concept of success.

The mayor does not have executive power over many of the levers needed to tackle these issues but does have an unparalleled platform and profile with which to tell a different story about politics and about our city, to challenge the received wisdom on inequality and to unite us behind a different vision of a fairer, more equal London.

The mayor's role lends itself to that of an activist: bringing their profile and pressure to bear, speaking with democratic legitimacy on areas over which he or she lacks executive responsibility. If they can embrace this role, maintaining respect and promoting unity wherever possible but never being afraid to challenge power if necessary, London's next mayor could transform our city and set a new route for national politics too; demonstrating that this principled alternative to the orthodoxy is possible could unleash national politics to do the same.

# 5

## A HEALTHY CITY

### DOING NO HARM

In 1858, MPs sitting in the House of Commons were so overcome by the stench of the sewage-ridden Thames flowing past Parliament that they hung enormous vinegar-soaked sheets over the windows to ward off the smell long enough for everyone to vote. Propelled into action by the nasal assault, they quickly found an enormous £3 million for an unprecedented overhaul of London's sewer system.[183] It has survived to this day.

That investment formed part of the late-nineteenth-century transformation of London's public infrastructure, motivated by a desire for the good health of the city and the recognition that this was a proper concern for government, helped along by the most visceral manifestation of the problem flowing right past the workplace of the UK's legislators. Pipes and sewers, regulations on food inspection, burial and the safety of buildings and public places eradicated diseases like cholera, vastly improved life expectancy and transformed London's environment. Those vinegar-soaked sheets came down, never to be put back up.

We take these functions for granted now. They are maintained by the quiet but vital work of professionals monitoring our water supply, ensuring the safe disposal of sewage, chasing down infectious diseases, checking our food is safe to eat and our buildings safe to work in. Watching the ease with which deadly diseases like Ebola and cholera take hold elsewhere is the only way to truly appreciate their importance here. Public health solved, then?

Absolutely not. We might have tamed the microbial threats to our safety but that has simply revealed new challenges. Life for Londoners is healthier and safer than it was for our Victorian ancestors, but London is not a healthy place to live, even by the standards of our biggest city rivals around the world.

We have the highest rate of childhood obesity of any major city, and more than half the adult population are obese or overweight.[184] More than 1 million Londoners will experience mental ill health this year – the total economic and social costs of which are estimated at £26 billion annually.[86] And these issues disproportionately affect the poorest: those in some of the richest wards can live a full twenty-five years longer than those in the poorest.[6] London comes seventh out of fourteen in health rankings of global cities.[184]

This is not a chapter about the National Health Service. That vital institution is much loved for a reason – it mostly rescues us from the terrible consequences of poor health, but it does little to prevent us falling ill in the first place. Had the NHS existed in 1858 it would not have been tasked with sewer design, and had the money been diverted from tunnelling to extra beds for cholera patients we would remain the poorer and sicker for it today. About 80 per cent of the increase in life expectancy in the twentieth century was due to public health measures – only 20 per cent was thanks to medical services.[185]

But we do take inspiration from the doctors' famous oath: 'first, do no harm'. It seems like an underwhelming aim on first impression – not to cure or treat, or save, but to avoid making things worse. Yet, in this chapter we imagine how London as a city would look if it did no harm, and it is anything but underwhelming. For many, London is a harmful place: in the air we breathe, the food we eat, the violence we fear, the gap between the richest and poorest, and in much more, our city can be bad for us.

New York has become a public health Mecca for many over the last few years. Republican mayor Bloomberg's determined, evidence-driven assault on causes of ill health – cigarettes, trans-fats, sugary drinks, a lack of walking and cycling infrastructure – was regularly mocked and attacked by right-wing critics but hailed as revolutionary by public health professionals worldwide and led, over the course of his three terms, to a three-year increase in life expectancy, almost double the US average.[186] Can London's next mayor steal his crown, and help London become – in the words of the London Health Commission – the healthiest major global city?

A city that does no harm would be comprised of healthy communities where we all have the money, the home, the security, the relationships and the services to stay mentally and physical healthy. And it would be full of knowledgeable people who know how to keep things that way, spot the first signs of trouble and react in an emergency.

## HEALTHY COMMUNITIES

The major health challenges we face in London today – conditions like diabetes, heart disease, lung cancer and liver disease – are often called 'lifestyle' diseases, because they are brought on by poor diet, smoking or drinking or lack of exercise. The implication is clear: people chose the lifestyle they lead; if they get sick it's their own fault.

This is wrong. It doesn't recognise the way our circumstances and surroundings constrain our choices. Not having enough money to buy healthy food, not having the time or the safe routes to walk or cycle, being bombarded with advertising for unhealthy food and drink, not knowing your neighbours, or feeling intimidated to go out after dark. These are some of the factors that contribute to what should more properly be called 'environmental diseases'.

Look back 150 years. Washing your hands and drinking clean water largely prevent cholera. Yet pioneering nineteenth-century leaders didn't put advisory stickers on polluted water pumps; they built sewers, decent housing and public infrastructure to provide clean water. They didn't just urge people to wash their hands; they removed the tax on soap. And to round up the laggards they introduced legislation to enforce sanitation standards on housing and public works.

Many of today's public health efforts seem disappointingly unambitious – tacitly accepting the 'lifestyle disease' hypothesis as they resort to advertising campaigns and information leaflets. There is certainly a role for information, and we cover it below. But good health stems first and foremost from the nature of the communities we live in. This section explores what needs to change.

## Tackle Inequality

Overwhelmingly, our city's richest live longer and healthier lives than the poorest. In the extreme this gap in life expectancy can extend to twenty-five years.[6] In thirty minutes or so you could travel along the Jubilee Line from Green Park (life expectancy at birth: ninety years) to Stratford (life expectancy: seventy-nine).[187] The Japanese are the healthiest nation in the world, in terms of life expectancy, and yet London's richest outlive them;[6] our poorest citizens, on the other hand, have a similar life expectancy to the people of Guatemala, ranked 143rd.[188]

As Pete Baker explained,[189] 'Poverty exposes people to health threats such as poor housing and low quality food. Poverty also causes psychological and social stress, which results in poorer mental and physical well-being ... and poverty makes it practically and psychologically more difficult to adopt healthy behaviours, resulting in people smoking more, eating less healthily and doing less exercise.'

But this inequality is not just a problem for the poor. 'Income inequality harms not only the health of those on low incomes, but also the health of the whole population, including the rich... This is partly because there is less social stress in equal societies but also because equal societies make a whole series of better collective decisions ... on provision of healthcare, on acceptable levels of air pollution, on provision of green parks and good cycle lanes.'

Richard Wilkinson and Kate Pickett – specialists in public health and authors of the book *The Spirit Level*[190] – have calculated that reducing inequality in London to Nordic and Japanese levels would halve obesity, cut mental illness by two-thirds and teenage births by nearly three-quarters. Trust levels would nearly double.[147]

In previous chapters we have covered a whole series of measures to tackle inequality in London, from raising the minimum wage to instituting company pay ratios, from creating new council tax bands to encouraging stronger unions. Quite apart from all the other benefits, were they to be successful they would yield a dramatic improvement in our collective health. Kate Pickett has called the living wage 'the single best action that ... local authorities can take to reduce health inequalities'.[191] And Andrew Attfield, writing on Changing London,[192] suggested that one of the most important things his east London hospital was doing to tackle health inequalities was actually nothing to do with healthcare at all – it was to create new, well-paid routes into NHS jobs for young people from the local area who might otherwise be struggling to find good work: 'The mayor should demand a minimum number of posts that are designated as apprenticeships and training positions and monitor the amount of local employment by larger employers.'

A more equal London would be a healthier London.

## Promote Friendly Communities and Good Neighbours

The modern version of the Hippocratic oath has this lovely pledge: 'I will remember that there is art to medicine as well as science, and that warmth, sympathy, and understanding may outweigh the surgeon's knife or the chemist's drug.'[193]

In Charlie Leadbeater's paper for the Centre for London, he argues that successful cities need both good systems and high empathy.[194] The distinction works well when thinking about our health. We need the systems – good healthcare, clean transport, green space, healthy food, secure housing, decent pay – but we also need the empathy that holds it all together – the warmth, sympathy and understanding that help us recover but even more importantly keep us healthy in the first place.

Studies have shown that severe loneliness is as detrimental to health as smoking fifteen cigarettes a day.[195] Living in a supportive community increases our chance of good health by 27 per cent.[68] Whether it's having someone to turn to in a crisis, feeling safer when you walk outside, or just the everyday boost to well-being of speaking with friends, family and neighbours, other people are good for our health. Yet, in London, one-quarter of our 9 million inhabitants describe themselves as feeling lonely often or all of the time.[4] It can become a spiral, with loneliness exacerbating mental illness and mental illness itself a cause of loneliness.

In Chapter 3 we described how a neighbourly city would function. We suggested streets and neighbourhoods designed so people could get to know each other, with cars shut out or slowed right down, a right to demand meeting spaces from local public agencies, local Plotting Sheds, locally delivered services, a time-based currency and much more. They will be just as vital to a healthy city as a good GP, access to healthy food, regular exercise or reduced air pollution.

## Help Us Cycle and Walk

Our increasingly sedentary lifestyles are taking their toll on our health: 1.8 million adults report doing less than thirty minutes moderately intense physical activity each week, yet higher activity levels could prevent 4100 deaths per year. Only 13 per cent of Londoners currently cycle or walk to work, despite half living close to their workplace.[184]

As well as the physical benefits of exercise, evidence suggests that simply getting out of the car will make people happier – Matthew Smerdon[196] reported on the researchers who convinced volunteers in England to wear electrode caps during their commutes and found that whether they were driving or taking the train, peak-hour travellers suffered worse stress than fighter pilots or riot police facing mobs of angry protesters.[197]

Many of these trips are unnecessary. TfL estimate that, every day, 4.5 million car trips (out of a total of 10 million) could be switched to walking, even taking into account people's age, the time of day, heavy loads and of course the distance (they're all under 2 km). One million bus trips (out of 6 million) could instead be walked.[198] We could be exercising more and polluting less.

## (1) Better, Safer Routes for Cycling and Walking

Concern about safety on the roads is the most significant reason people give for not cycling in London.[199] And three-quarters of Londoners said that improved safety and security would encourage them to walk more (particularly if they knew it was quicker than the bus).[200]

Other comparable cities are proof that it is possible: in London 8 per cent of people commute by bike; in Copenhagen the figure is 50 per cent.[184] A comprehensive network of safe cycle routes separated from the traffic guides cyclists around the city. Groningen – allegedly the most bike-friendly city in the world – divided itself into quarters and banned cars from travelling between them, forcing vehicles out onto the ring road and clearing the roads for bikes.[201] Every Sunday Bogotá's Ciclovia sees the city close 75 km of its roads to traffic, leaving them free for two million riotous cyclists, walkers, street performers and skaters.[202]

Closer to home, Bristol's popular Making Sundays Special events see the centre of the city closed off to traffic on summer Sundays.[37] And even in London, until recently, one day near Christmas was dubbed Very Important Pedestrian Day by the businesses of the West End; cars were shut out and pedestrians headed for the shops unimpeded.[203]

Unlike most of the issues we have covered in this book, this is one over which the mayor does have some direct, budgetary control. It is ironic, then, that while portraying himself as a campaigner for cycling, Boris Johnson has presided over a city that continues to prioritise the car: London's Green Party pointed out last year that his plans for transport investment to 2050 see £28 billion earmarked for roads and only £1 billion for cycling infrastructure.[204]

In one of the few areas where the mayor does actually have power over a substantial budget, giving a good speech is not enough; he or she must change the policy too.

## (2) Encourage Walking to Work

Improvements in infrastructure and changes to the built environment will transform opportunities for safer, healthier transport but there is room too for subtler efforts. The London Health Commission recommends harnessing London's businesses to the cause. Employee ill health costs business dear and efforts elsewhere have shown that employees can be incentivised to commute more healthily. They recommend a 'walk the last mile to work and the first mile back' scheme, jointly promoted by TfL and employers, whereby workers receive travel incentives if their Oyster card history shows they start walking at least a mile before they arrive at work in the morning, and don't step back onto the tube until they're a mile from work in the evening. In a similar vein the commission recommends more systematic encouragement to take the stairs rather than the lift and suggest that 'stand on the right' signs on tube escalators should be replaced with 'walk on the left' to nudge people into walking up.

## (3) Shorten the Commute

In 1987 only 9 per cent of Londoners took more than an hour to get to work. Today, despite faster trains and enormous investment in road-building, more than a quarter of us (28 per cent) commute for longer than an hour.[21] Travelling these distances is bad for the traveller and it's bad for our lungs, it clogs our streets, kills our cyclists and robs us of free time. Matthew Smerdon argued[205] that ultimately 'we need to live closer to the places we need to go. And the places we need to go need to be closer to where we live.' A city that does no harm would be planned very differently, and although this isn't a job that a mayor could complete in a single term it is one that we think he or she has a duty to lead.

## Clean the Air

In the nineteenth century, it was sewage running through the streets of London that made people ill; in the twenty-first century, cars and trucks have taken its place. David Christie[206] contrasted the 153 people killed in road accidents in 2012 with the estimated 4500 who died from the effects of air pollution. Despite Mayor Johnson's protestations of innocence, London is so far in breach of what are deemed safe limits for some pollutants that we face paying hundreds of millions of pounds in fines to the EU over the next few years.[207] The back of a car is now far more dangerous than the front.

Replacing car and bus journeys with cycling and walking is likely to be an essential part of the campaign to curb London's dangerous levels of air pollution – in parts of central London, road transport is responsible for around 80 per cent of airborne pollution, with black cabs contributing 30 per cent of particulate matter emissions in the area[151] – but insufficient on its own. The emissions of those vehicles left on the road, and the other sources of air pollution, must be brought under control too.

Other cities have tried all sorts of innovative ways to tackle the problem. After dangerous smog had engulfed Paris for the fifth consecutive day in 2014, the French government ordered all cars with a number plate ending in an even number to stay at home. Seven hundred extra police flooded onto the streets to issue €22 fines to anyone caught defying the ban, and public transport was made temporarily free. The next day, as pollution levels dropped sharply, the ban was lifted and the ecology minister declared 'Bravo, and thank you'.[208]

This drastic lottery-based approach to curbing car use in major cities smacks of desperation but in some urban areas it is a weekly or even daily occurrence. In Mexico City, every car is banned from the roads for one day each week, based on its number plate. The result, unfortunately, has been a rise in pollution over the long term, as people have increasingly bought cheap, inefficient second cars with carefully chosen number plates to circumvent the ban. In Bogotá a similar scheme operates during peak traffic hours, but rather than seek alternatives to their cars, drivers simply travelled more during off-peak times, or drove further to avoid the restricted zones.[208]

Other efforts have been more successful. Unlike London's Low Emission Zone – which only applies to buses, lorries and coaches

– Stockholm's covers all private vehicles and is far more ambitious. Diesel is banned completely (diesel fumes are far more harmful than petrol emissions) and petrol cars have to meet strict limits. The same is true in Berlin, which has seen a considerable fall in pollution levels.[208] Meanwhile, Beijing is amongst the most polluted cities in the world. Having successfully, but only temporarily, reduced pollution during the Olympics through strict car bans and shutting most of the city's factories, the government has now devoted an astonishing 760 billion yuan (£75.8 billion) to improve the city's air quality by 2017, including through stopping coal burning in industry and enforcing cleaner car emissions.[209] The measures include spending £5 billion on new trees alone.

In Oslo, electric charging points have infiltrated most neighbourhoods, with aggressive tax breaks and other financial incentives worth an estimated £5000 a year designed to tempt people into ditching diesel and petrol. Norway is the first country in the world where 1 in 100 cars are electric.[210]

David Christie outlined what we could be doing in London: 'The air quality strategy already sets out measures we can use such as stricter limits for the London Low Emission Zone and ensuring all taxis and buses in London use clean technology. We can target poor air quality hotspots, promote low-emission vehicles and retrofit others to be less polluting.'

This is an area where solutions are not hard to find, but matching rhetoric with action is much harder. The congestion charge was bold and ground-breaking in its day and one of the few examples of truly transformative London mayoral policies. It's time to repeat the trick.

## Make London Safe

Violence and the threat of violence damage our health and well-being. A city that did no harm would be one in which we all felt safe and free from harassment. Even though crime is falling in London – by 6 per cent last year – domestic violence seems to be on the rise and too many people are still victims or are fearful of becoming so.[211] It affects our health and quality of life.

Young women from the MsUnderstood Partnership contributed to Changing London[212] and reported that 'The issue of feeling unsafe, at risk and meeting harm is something each of us have individually experienced a considerable number of times.'

For women, particularly, London can be a threatening or dangerous city. Almost 50,000 incidences of domestic violence were reported to the police in London in 2012/13 (and nationally only 20 per cent of cases are reported, suggesting the figure could be five times that). Between 50 and 60 per cent of female mental health service users have experienced domestic violence. One in three 16–18-year-old girls reported unwanted sexual touching at school. Thirty-one per cent of women aged 18–24 report experiencing unwanted sexual attention on London public transport, and 41 per cent of those aged between 18 and 34 have experienced it in public places.[213]

The MsUnderstood Partnership recommended some practical steps to ensure that women and girls feel safer, particularly after dark: more trusted workers from charities and women's organisations on the streets to help with information and support; better street lighting and CCTV; and a new TfL app which allows you to text trusted contacts your route home and expected arrival time.

They are clear, though, that this must take place as part of a wider preventative campaign against violence and harassment, including: 'Compulsory sex-and-relationships education in schools and preventative campaigns which focus on the attitudes young people develop in terms of masculinity, femininity and respect. Further work involving trusted local business and community groups is also essential for transforming our local neighbourhoods and making them safer.'

This is an issue on which the mayor – man or woman – could take a high-profile lead role.

The former mayor of Bogotá Antanas Mockus understood that women were afraid to go out at night in the city. He said: 'At that time, we were also looking for what would be the best image of a safe city, and I realized that if you see streets with many women you feel safer.'[214] He organised a series of 'nights for women' which saw

700,000 women attend free concerts and bar nights and take over the city centre. Most men complied with the voluntary curfew and stayed at home to look after the kids, and those that didn't carried a 'pass of good conduct' to explain why they were out on the streets. The streets were patrolled by 1500 women police officers, and Mayor Mockus spent the evening at home playing with his four-year-old daughter. Another Colombian city repeated the event earlier this year.[215] Not a solution on its own of course, but a powerful signal of how our city could be different.

## Tackle the Fear of Crime

About 30 per cent of Londoners say they are worried or very worried about crime in their area.[216] Fear of crime is associated with poorer mental health, reduced physical activity and a lower quality of life. People reporting that they were more afraid of crime took less exercise, saw friends less often and took part in fewer social activities.[217]

Kate Jopling[218] wrote about the effect it has on loneliness among older people: 'Many older people feel like prisoners in their own homes after nightfall – and the long winter nights can be a breeding ground for loneliness. Older people's fear of crime may be disproportionate to their risk, but this cannot be an excuse for failure to act to address it. Community policing teams need to take responsibility for identifying and supporting older people to feel able to take an active part in community life.'

Amongst young people, guns, gangs and knives are a major cause of feeling unsafe. Although gang crime went down by 23 per cent last year, there were still almost 1000 incidences of young people being assaulted with either a gun or a knife in 2013. Gang members themselves are most at risk: 61 per cent have been a victim of crime.[219] But the fear can spread through communities of those not directly involved. A peaceful city would continue the successful work to reduce gang crime, and work with communities to reduce the fear of crime among young people.

## Promote Healthy Food

When asked what should be the priority for improving the city's health, reducing the number of fast food outlets came (just) top of Londoner's demands.[220]

Our diet, even more so than our lack of exercise, has left us with the highest rate of childhood obesity of any city in the world; and 3.8 million of us are overweight or obese – more than half the adult population.[184] The dangers of obesity are well known, and the London Health Commission put them more starkly than most: 'It raises the risk of serious physical health conditions such as diabetes, heart disease, stroke and cancer. It drains energy during the day and causes sleeplessness at night. It affects our mental health too – our sense of self-esteem and happiness – and can stop us from leading the lives that we want and fulfilling our dreams for ourselves and our families.'

On Changing London, Esther Murray explained:[221] 'When children are adequately nourished they concentrate better at school, learn better, play better and sleep better.' Tahseen and Aisha Chowdhury[222] looked in detail at just one illness associated strongly with obesity: diabetes. It now accounts for 10 per cent of the UK's healthcare spending, and one in five beds at the Royal London Hospital – where Tahseen is a doctor – are occupied by people with the condition. Healthier diets and more exercise would reduce obesity and therefore diabetes far more cheaply than it can be treated.

Crucially, like exercise, our diet is a product of our surroundings as much as a function of personal choice. London's next mayor should take the following steps.

## (1) Ban Fast Food Outlets Near Schools

The London Health Commission reports that London has 8000 fast food outlets, with the number increasing by 10 per cent a year. If one is located within 160 metres of a school, obesity rises by 5 per cent. Tahseen and Aisha find that 'it is a common, if uncomfortable, sight to see queues of children outside fried chicken joints at the end of school'.

The power to approve fast food outlets rests with local authorities, and although most have been reticent to interfere, Waltham Forest has recently led the way, refusing 82 per cent of fast food outlets and asserting that planning permission will usually be refused for shops within ten minutes walk of schools, parks and youth centres.[184] Other east London councils have followed suit. The London Health Commission recommends considerably bolstered support from the mayor's office, with the next London Plan stipulating that fast food shops will have to prove they will have no impact on health if they're proposing setting up within 400 metres of a school. In public polling for the commission, 73 per cent supported the idea.

This last loophole would allow a way in for innovative solutions like Shift's Box Chicken project,[223] which tries to provide a healthier and competitively priced alternative. Another option might be to try and impose calorie limits on those shops that do want to set up near schools (e.g. changing the type of oil used can make a difference). As Shift recognises, the chicken shop is as much a social setting as a food shop.

## (2) Lobby for a Sugar Tax

Lord Darzi – Chairman of the London Health Commission – has made the case for a national sugar tax. It is not within the London mayor's powers to impose, but he or she should lobby for it within government. It also has international precedent: France, Denmark, Hungary and Mexico have all introduced taxes on sugar-sweetened drinks.[184]

## Ban Smoking in Public Places Outdoors, Including Outside Hospitals

A healthy community would be smoke free. More than 8000 Londoners die prematurely every year from illnesses caused by smoking – it's the highest single cause of death. And despite successful public health interventions like the ban on smoking in enclosed public spaces, there are still 1.2 million smokers in London, disproportionately concentrated in the poorest boroughs. An average of sixty-seven London children take up smoking every day, and, of course, once addicted it's extremely difficult to quit.[184]

For global cities, London's 18 per cent smoking prevalence ranks it about midway between the worst performing (Paris on 40 per cent) and the best (Hong Kong on 13 per cent). But this disguises significant variation by borough, with rates rising to 24 per cent in the worst affected. Hong Kong and New York have led the way, banning smoking in public areas (including outside) and seeing dramatic falls in smoking rates. New York's efforts are thought to have prevented 55,000 early deaths.[184]

The London Health Commission recently recommended the mayor work with councils to ban smoking in all public parks and outdoor public spaces, like Trafalgar Square.

Writing on Changing London, Andrew Attfield[224] reported on the efforts of the east London hospital where he works to ban smoking in its grounds. He emphasised the importance of offering support alongside new regulation, to help those who want to quit. He recommends 'A strategic planning requirement for a smoke free area within 50 metres of a hospital entrance would give a clear message, especially if reinforced by ... consistent support to help smokers give up.'

## Build Decent Housing

The clear link between bad housing and poor health has been apparent since Victorian times, and we now know that 'inadequate housing is associated with increased bronchitis, pneumonia, stroke, heart disease and accidents, for example, while overcrowding is associated with infections, stress and intra-family violence.'[225]

We have covered housing design in previous chapters and others have done so in far more detail than we can. Nonetheless, this focus on the health impacts of housing should require that we don't chase quantity at the expense of quality – the new houses we undoubtedly need must be designed and built to bolster good health rather than undermine it.

# KNOWLEDGEABLE PEOPLE

Asked whether they wanted to lead a healthier lifestyle – eating better, exercising more, limiting smoking and drinking – 80–90 per cent of Londoners consistently said they were quite willing or very willing to do so.[220] There is an appetite for information on how to live more healthily. It can be a powerful complement to the changes in our environment outlined above.

## Tackle Mental Health Stigma

One in four people have mental health problems – more than voted for Boris Johnson in the last mayoral election.[86] Add in the friends and family that are also impacted and that's more than voted for all the candidates put together. And if one considers the £26 billion annual cost of mental health problems,[86] it's a mystery why political campaigns stay so quiet on one of the most important public health issues facing our city.

As Sarah Holloway argued,[226] the mayor might not have direct control over mental health services but that doesn't matter: 'everything listed under the mayoral remit, from planning and development to housing and transport, all have major implications for our mental health.' They are explored throughout the book.

But mental health campaigners have also long stressed the need to tackle public and official ignorance, which worsens the experience for those suffering mental illness and helps cause and perpetuate it. Marion Janner speaks from years of experience:[227] 'The fact that mental illness is invisible makes it even more important that warm, supportive, unpatronising help is loudly publicised.'

She argues that 'the best thing a new mayor could do would be to speak openly and unsqueamishly about mental illness. They have a powerful effect as a role-model in addition to their direct power as an employer and budget-holder.' Even better, 'if the mayor happened to have direct experience of mental illness and felt able to be open about this, that would be amazing!'

Marion described the everyday challenge of navigating London with borderline personality disorder: when a seat on the tube for her and support dog Buddy, or help from TfL and shop staff, would transform the experience. She suggested training for staff in how to support people with 'hidden' disabilities, clear indication that they're willing to help, and a more generic version of the 'baby on board' badge.

Liz Meek revealed that London is the schizophrenia capital of the UK.[228] People with schizophrenia die twenty years younger than the general population. Only 8 per cent of people with schizophrenia and other psychotic illnesses work, but many more would like to, and there are tried-and-tested ways of successfully supporting people back into work. She suggested we raise that figure from 8 per cent to 25 per cent in ten years. Better community services would dramatically improve people's care. And tackling the stigma associated with mental illness would transform the quality of life of sufferers.

Mayor Johnson pledged his support on World Mental Health Day last year and the GLA released a major report on the costs of mental ill health. Mental health is a priority for the London Health Board, which the mayor chairs. But it is loud, high-profile public support that the issue needs most from the mayor. He or she could become the face of the Time to Change campaign in London, make it the centrepiece of their election campaign and one of the driving themes of their mayoralty. It would be unconventional – mental health rarely features prominently in political campaigns – but with one in four directly affected by mental illness, and their friends and family no doubt impacted too, it would not just be the right thing to do, but good politics too.

## Introduce Health Traffic Lights on Restaurant Food

New York's former mayor Bloomberg has waged a high-profile battle against sugary and fatty foods. He banned artificial trans-fats from restaurant food (which saw big chains like McDonalds alter their recipes rather than lose their New York trade) and compelled chains to display calorie counts on their menus. Only latterly, in his attempt to ban the sale of supersize fizzy drinks, did he come unstuck when the court ruled he didn't have the power.[186]

Giving people more information about the calories contained in restaurant food will never be enough on its own, but it could help nudge people into healthier choices at the margins. The London Health Commission suggests a traffic light system mandated in chain restaurants, summarising the fat, salt and calorie content of dishes.

## Learn the Signs and Symptoms of Cancer

Too many of us don't know how to identify the early signs and symptoms of common cancers, even though one in three people gets cancer during their lives.[229] Evidence shows that this works: people who know what to look out for, and who are confident going for screening, are more likely to have cancers detected early when they're still treatable, ultimately prolonging their lives.

Frances Clarke suggested[230] a Save Ourselves Day to spread awareness of the signs and symptoms of cancer and the importance of screening: 'led by the mayor with promotion going out to all employees starting with the public sector and then onto the private. Information to be shared in schools, colleges and universities, messages on the intercom at underground stations, simple messages that everyone can understand.'

The ongoing effort could draw in much of the public sector beyond the NHS. When we reach pensionable age we simultaneously become eligible for TfL's Freedom Pass, entitling us to free travel around the city, and for a free bowel cancer screening. The first is more popular than the second. Frances suggests including information about the cancer screening in communications about the Freedom Pass, perhaps alongside some advertising about the health benefits of getting out and about with the new freedom afforded by free travel. The Freedom Pass application process is online – perhaps an opportunity for an intergenerational project to offer help to those aged sixty-plus who need it to make the application, alongside a brief explanation of the screening process. The possibilities for these kinds of projects multiply once you begin to make the links. A good mayor would do just that.

## Make Sure We All Know First Aid

St Johns Ambulance say that approximately 140,000 people die every year in the UK in situations where their lives could have been saved if somebody had known first aid.[231] Assuming that distribution is very roughly even, those figures translate into somewhere between ten and fifteen lives lost unnecessarily in every London borough every week.

Janani Arulrajah[232] outlined on Changing London the importance of first aid training and suggested making it available to all Londoners. Ensuring first aid is on the school curriculum for every child would get us all off to a good start, although reasonably regular refresher training is important in adulthood so we don't forget it all immediately. Employers are required to have a minimum number of trained first aiders but it would not add much to the training budget to ensure everyone knew how to react in an emergency.

## Do All This Together, in a Save Ourselves Week

Frances suggested a Save Ourselves Day but perhaps a week would give more chance to reach more people about more issues. Simple messages about a few important topics: cancer, first aid, mental health and food; disseminated via workplaces, schools, public transport, the media and online.

Save Ourselves Week would be an important part of the London Calendar we suggested in Chapter 3; coordinating city-wide efforts on all sorts of areas – from work-experience opportunities to opening up our arts institutions to young people.

Vital knowledge about our own health could also form part of the Have-a-Go Festival we suggested in the second chapter: 'an annual festival where we all take part: act on the stage, sing at the O2, play at Wembley, paint at the Tate... Have a go at riding a bike for the first time, at learning to swim, at ballroom dancing, at being a first aider.'

However it is done, creating moments with two or three such focal points every year could excite and incentivise every participant, every contributor, potentially every Londoner with the feeling that they were part of something bigger than themselves. Maybe making a date provides the opportunity, the discipline, the excuse – the pressure even – to do the things we know we should but we've never quite got round to doing in the past, like checking for cancer or learning first aid?

## LAST WORDS: A ROLE FOR LEADERSHIP

The mayor set up the London Health Commission last year to report on what London should do to become the world's healthiest major city. It published its excellent final report last autumn, and we've adopted several of the ideas in this chapter.

The overriding impression is that London punches below its weight in health policy. Compared with other world cities we are less healthy and – perhaps because London government has no responsibility for health services – there is very little high-profile pan-London leadership, including from the mayor.

This need not be the case. Firstly because many of the areas over which the mayor does have responsibility or influence – roads, pavements and cycle paths, policing, housing, public parks, planning, air pollution and many more – are vital to good mental and physical health. And secondly because what's lacking in many cases is not the ideas but the leadership to coordinate and pull together disparate schemes scattered around various public agencies.

The overweight Oklahoma City mayor Mick Cornett led his whole city on a campaign to 'lose a million pounds' with huge success and an impact well beyond the waistline. Nothing was overlooked, from developing a 'health focused streetscape' to encouraging restaurateurs to introduce new menus. Above all, Mayor Cornett set a personal example. Now the city is not only fitter and leaner, but low healthcare costs and diminishing workplace absentee rates have attracted unprecedented investment; last year unemployment was down to just 4.5 per cent and Oklahoma City boasted the strongest economy of any major metropolitan area in the US.[233]

Could our next mayor bring about a similar transformation in the health of Londoners? The effort would involve far more than the NHS, and the effects would ripple well beyond the health statistics themselves. A transformation on this scale will require a generation to take hold but the leadership and the commitment are necessary now and much can be achieved even in a five-year term. Nineteenth-century boldness transformed the city; London's next mayor has the chance to transform it again.

# 6

# A Deeper Democracy

## Being and Doing

Lord Healey once said that chancellors must do something; prime ministers must be something.[234] Mayors, we think, must do and be.

Other chapters have been about what the next mayor might do to make London 'a great place to grow up', for instance, or 'a city of thriving neighbourhoods'. This chapter focuses on how they might do these things and others. It is about effective leadership and about re-tooling democracy for the twenty-first century.

We think our next leader must be willing to listen, determined to collaborate and proudly committed to clearly set out, democratically endorsed and consistently upheld values. We imagine a city that is governed by the principles of its mayor and that, within that framework, provides opportunities for all its citizens to be involved in planning, choosing and delivering.

Londoners voting for values and delivering them together.

We explore some ways in which this might play out on the ground and we suggest that this deepening of democracy is, now more than ever, necessary and important. We also think that a mayoral candidate offering this approach to leadership in 2016 would be smart politics.

London is no powder keg – not least because the lonely, the mentally ill and the very poor are an improbable insurgency – but, as we have seen, it is a city of appearances. For all its wealth, its long and settled history and its advanced infrastructure, there are troubling fault lines, largely unattended, and just below the surface.

Even those who aren't struggling may still be amongst the one in three who worry about crime on the streets[216] and will certainly be paying their share of the £26 billion that is, according to the GLA, the annual total economic and social cost of mental ill health in London.[86] The costs of dysfunction are borne by us all.

We think the next mayor could transform London or, better still, help us to work on changing it together, but transformational politicians need popular support and barely one in three voted in the 2012 mayoral election, with the vote topping half the electorate in just two wards and dropping to less than 20 per cent elsewhere in the capital.[235] London may not have reached the position of Chişinău, the capital of Moldova, where the most recent mayoral elections had to be repeated three times due to lack of interest,[236] but we are heading in the wrong direction. Overall turnout in 2012 was 16 per cent lower than in the previous election for the London mayor.

Democracy only works when the voters believe that it can. An enfeebled mandate means a weaker mayor, and a weak mayor undermines the faith yet further.

We could do better: the Scottish referendum has shown the potential of a different approach. Here voters relished serious debate and active participation in the decisions that will affect their lives. Towards the end of a vibrant two-year discussion, the politicians were no longer dictating the terms of the debate; the people were deciding, in very large numbers, and for once in modern politics in the UK the dog was wagging the tail.

In the immediate aftermath, national politicians seemed to recognise an appetite for the devolution of powers away from Westminster and Whitehall and towards the regions, and maybe also the big cities. This debate has barely begun, and is to be encouraged, but we think it represents only half of the learning from the Scottish experience.

The results of the vote revealed an appetite for devolution. The level of engagement, in the campaign as well as in the vote itself, revealed an appetite for democratic participation. Both are important and, to a certain extent, participation should be expected to flow from devolution, but this is not inevitable or automatic.

The first element, challenging though it is, may be easier to satisfy than the second, but we won't engage Londoners and we won't tackle London's problems if the next mayoral election offers no more than a dreary parade of top-down, patronisingly short, infinitesimally differentiated, bog-standard political retail campaigns. Our democracy here is ephemeral and paper thin.

This mattered before the Scottish referendum; now it matters even more. Judging from the Westminster rhetoric it seems possible that a ripple of devolution will soon be coursing down the Thames and depositing new powers on the next mayor. They need, and we need, a deeper democracy, retooled for 2016.

## Retooling Democracy for 2016

We suggest that three insights must inform the approach of the next mayor.

First, the world has changed since the mayoralty was established. The internet sensibility, as much its technical capability, has infected every aspect of our lives. We want to be involved as equals in the 'development of content', to be seen and heard in every aspect of our lives. Engaging with this horizontal world demands a far deeper sensitivity, awareness of individual agency and willingness to actively distribute responsibility than UK politicians have contemplated in the past.

This isn't about a mayoral tweet now and then or the occasional online survey from party headquarters. It is – as Neal Lawson noted in *The Guardian*[237] and on the first day of Changing London[238] – far more fundamental: 'People will stop being the occasional consumers of politics and instead become its permanent producers'; `The test of the next mayor's radicalism will not be the agenda they dictate but how effectively they empower the people of London to collectively transform our city.'

Second, leading a city is different from leading a borough or a country. As we noted in Chapter 1, cities are big enough to make a difference on issues that are too large for towns and boroughs but also small enough to be more adventurous than nation states: more nimble, more imaginative and much more ambitious. They can achieve different things, big things.

Third, most of what happens in London isn't run by the mayor. They can indeed do big things, but not on their own.

It follows from these precepts that an ambitious mayor should...

## Be Willing to Listen

'Citizens are the mayor', says Seoul's Park Won-Soon. One of his first acts after entering office was to install a giant statue of an ear outside City Hall.[239] 'No one great genius can lead a city', he said, 'instead citizens need to lead, and my job is to get their ideas into the system.'

Some ideas transfer better than others. We don't think a 'Big Ear' on Queen Elizabeth Walk would necessarily attract a helpful response, but we can see very clearly that an appetite for listening has been a common hallmark of some of the most successful mayors around the world

## Be Determined to Collaborate

The success factors underpinning effective social change projects, ranging in scope from the reduction of teenage binge drinking in Massachusetts to the tackling of homelessness in Calgary, have been examined by Fay Hanleybrown, John Kania and Mark Kramer.[240] Their conclusion is unequivocal: 'The most critical factor by far is an influential champion ... one who is passionately focused on solving a problem but willing to let the participants figure out the answers for themselves.'

This is what we mean by a collaborative mayor: one whose leadership draws people together in pursuit of a common cause and who brings out the best in everyone. Convening, inspiring and driving, sharing credit, but not doing everything.

## Be Committed to Rock Solid Values, Consistently Upheld

There is a risk in working closely with others: collaboration can obfuscate, diminish and delay. Collaborative leadership is purposeful leadership only when the goals are clear and based on principles that are evident to everyone. The keen-listening, well-respected collaborator only becomes a great leader and not an aimless follower when the contribution of the many is shaped by, and mediated through, a distinctive set of rock solid, proudly promoted, democratically endorsed and consistently upheld values.

Watching the hordes rush past his window, French revolutionary leader Ledru-Rollin was famously supposed to have said: 'There go the people. I must follow them, for I am their leader.'[241] Today, focus groups and opinion polls chase past the gaze of our political leaders to similar effect. Following is easy but contributors to Changing London called for more. They want a mayoral programme that sets a new course. They want it to be bold and individual and they want strong and explicit principles to be the essence of the distinction. They want to vote for values.

'For all and first for the poor' was the simple mantra of Mexico City mayor López Obrador.[242] Some will foresee dire consequences if such an approach is adopted in London but this will be what New York's Mayor de Blasio has called 'the lazy logic of false choice politics'. This is the belief that 'prosperity can't be both great, and shared... That you can't lift the floor for those struggling in a tough economy, and still balance a budget... That those of us who serve can't expect to achieve anything at all if we dare to advance policies that are bold and morally right.'[12] The recognition that we sink or swim together and that ultimately a bias towards the poor would benefit us all has been at the heart of Changing London and must, we think, be the pole star for the next London mayor.

'There has to be a recognition', wrote John Tizard shortly after the Scottish referendum, 'that politics and political practices have to change given how much people feel alienated and disempowered. Such a settlement and relevant political practices have to be value-based and driven by the kind of society and economy we wish to live in. For me that means a fairer, more equal, cohesive and inclusive, and socially just society underpinned by a fairer more socially responsible economy; and a political system based on equal access and inclusiveness, high levels of engagement, transparency, accountability and social purpose.'[243]

We will return to the political as well as the moral argument for this position at the end of this chapter and we deal with some of the specifics in other chapters, but it is sufficient for now to note the importance of clearly understood, democratically endorsed and consistently upheld values, upfront and centre stage.

## DRAW FROM THE WISDOM OF THE CITY

### Set Up 'Ideas for London'

It is with imagination, wrote Emily Dickinson, that we light the slow fuse of the possible.[244] By sharing ideas, learning from one another and knocking suggestions together we break new ground and feel a collective sense of ownership for the outcome. We already have Transport for London and Homes for London, we suggest an addition: Ideas for London (IfL) – dedicated to unearthing and developing great new ideas from London's citizens and friends from other cities across the globe.

Several mayors around the world have found new ways of drawing on the wisdom of their city. In Vienna, 8500 people took part in 600 two-hour-long 'Charter Talks' to define a collective vision for parks, schools, churches, companies and apartment buildings throughout the city.[90]

Starting in 1999, Washington's mayor has held a series of 'Citizens Summits' each year with thousands of participants, voting on their priorities for city spending and policy. They were so successful that they were reintroduced by a subsequent mayor in 2013.[245] Mexico City's mayor set up 'Laboratorio para la Ciudad' – a 'creative think tank' for the city – led by charismatic artist Gabriella Gómez-Mont with a mission to develop and test great new ideas for the city government.[246] IfL would generate, gather and develop the ideas of Londoners. At the minimum, IfL would take charge of the consultation processes necessary for new policy proposals, but it should go much further. It should provide mechanisms for individuals and groups to propose new ideas and for the rest of us to consider them.

It's likely that most suggestions would be relatively modest, improving an existing service or system, but an ambitious mayor would signal a special interest in, to borrow Google's vocabulary, a 'Moonshots' programme. Here we would be looking for radical ideas that offer a different approach to tackling a big issue. Governments, both local and national ones, aren't generally noted for daring innovation, although the opportunities are huge. The next mayor could usefully challenge that convention.

The process must be inclusive and provide a range of opportunities for participation. IfL might, for instance, coordinate, or at least link with, the Plotting Sheds envisaged by Julian Dobson in Chapter 3. In addition – and as we have begun in a very small way with Changing London – it would scour the earth for the best ideas.

Even ideas from the most surprising places can be transferable. For instance, the aforementioned Big Ear might not work so well in London, but did you know that the successful and very popular Baby on Board badges distributed to expectant mothers by Transport for London is copied from the same city: Seoul?[247] Successful mayors around the world are increasingly learning from one another and there is now a wealth of wisdom for IfL to draw upon in resources like the i-teams research project.[248]

An online platform for Londoners to contribute experience, opinion and suggestions would also be an obvious and important dimension. This needs to be more sophisticated than an off-the-shelf website, which is likely to attract only problems and complaints, if it attracts anything at all. The platform needs a thoughtful and imaginative structure building on the behavioural insights that have informed crowdsourcing sites in other places and contexts.

Some suggestions will still be inappropriate for the mayor's office – better addressed to the local authority or some other agency. Advising correspondents who to approach instead would also be a useful function of the online platform and would further help to oil the wheels of a participative democracy, not just in City Hall but across the capital.

Too often these kinds of mechanisms can feel like a black hole: you post your comment and hear no more. If participants don't feel that their contribution is going anywhere, they won't be making another one. IfL must therefore also include provision for effective tracking, reporting and feedback. This might be linked to the kind of measurement and evaluation process that we proposed in Chapter 3 as the function of the London Index.

Established at City Hall in the opening weeks of a new mayoralty, we suggest that, within the first 100 days, IfL would send a powerful message to the people of this city: consultation and engagement isn't just for elections, you don't need to wait another four years for a say in your home town, your insight is very important to the mayor and it's very important to London.

But this recommendation comes with a warning. Would-be mayors must ask themselves an important question: am I prepared to be really serious about consultation?

Consider the experience of politicians who have talked about the environment and are then found to be driving a gas guzzler, or leaders who have championed personal morality and then been caught with their pants down. Promising something and doing the opposite is worse than never promising it in the first place.

Consultation, like environmental awareness or personal morality sounds like an obviously good thing to do, and it is, but only if you are prepared to embrace it in your own behaviour, to work hard at engaging opinions, to spend time on the findings and to use the learning thoughtfully and openly. Our advice to the next mayor is: do it well. And if you can't do it well, don't do it at all.

## Lead the Development of Our Vision for London

'To make London the best place to work, live, play, study, invest, and do business' are the expansive and comprehensive 'ambitions for London' set out by Boris Johnson in his Vision 2020.[249] We found plenty to support but we still have a fundamental problem with Vision 2020: we didn't think of it.

This isn't quite as mean spirited as it sounds. To have a practical value, to inspire, to motivate and to mobilise, surely we need to feel some sense of ownership for this vision of our city, or at least some sense of connection. A vision that is dreamt up in City Hall and pushed out fully formed will attract media comment but no popular buy-in. The whole process will produce better results if it actively seeks, and is based on, the insights and contributions of the many.

We think the next mayor should lead the development of our vision for London – one that we imagine together: IfL should drive the process.

When he was elected in 2010, Julian Castro – up-and-coming Democrat star and new mayor of San Antonio – wanted to know how his citizens would define success; what would have to change in their city under his watch for them to think he had done a good job?

He was serious about this, too. No rushed, internal report accompanied by a few headline stats – he wanted a big vision backed up by detailed benchmarks against which he and the city could judge progress, and, crucially, they couldn't be dreamt up in City Hall but had to come directly from citizens themselves.

Castro set up San Antonio 2020 (SA2020), a process he chaired himself, with representatives from across the sectors in the city, and asked thousands of people at five large events, and online, what they dreamt of for their neighbourhood. These ideas were boiled down to eleven areas (e.g. education, family well-being, transport) and for each there were a set of core criteria that would define success.

He then spun off SA2020 into its own separate charity, with two jobs: to encourage citizens to help achieve the goals themselves (e.g. through volunteering) and to publish an annual report on how city government was doing, tracking each benchmark and scoring the mayor's progress.[250]

A vision for London, collaboratively developed, would set a direction for the city, allowing us all to hold the new mayor to account for what is promised. It would be bold, detailed and, most importantly, ours.

### Understand that Collaboration Involves Challenge as Well as Agreement

Imagining and planning together isn't just about agreeing to do new things. Sharing responsibility is also about challenging one another. We wonder, for example, what Londoners might have thought about the current mayor's enthusiasm for the Garden Bridge if they had known that a plan which was once expected to cost £60 million and to be funded entirely by private sponsorship is now costed at £175 million with, so far, £30 million coming from government and a further £30 million from London's coffers via Transport for London.[251] The commercial secretary to the Treasury, Lord Deighton, claims that a Garden Bridge delivers 'two things for the price of one – a garden and a bridge'.[252] Given that a garden of comparable size could be bought for less than £4 million and a pedestrian bridge proposed for Battersea is expected to cost £22 million,[253] we suspect that the Garden Bridge plan would not have been approved by an electorate that was involved in making choices and could do the adding up.

Planning together would have lots of benefits. Not least, it would save us from a vain mayor.

## SEEK OPINIONS ON COMPETING PRIORITIES
### Start the April Vote

Compare the turnout in the Scottish independence referendum with the number that voted in the last election for London mayor. More than double the share of eligible voters made their mark: 38 per cent in London, 84.5 per cent in Scotland.[254]

The Scottish referendum showed that voters can engage with political ideas that are more challenging than a soundbite, with debates that last longer than a three-week campaign and with a political process that genuinely shapes the future. As Neal Ascherson wrote in the *Observer*, the 'campaign wasn't about persuading people how to vote, but people persuading politicians'.[255]

This was something new. We saw that a referendum could be a mechanism not only for making a decision but also for promoting a debate and, through that debate, refining policy positions, even for developing new ones. And we saw how that discussion could awaken a wider interest in democratic participation: SNP membership almost quadrupled between the vote and the end of the year.[256]

How might this learning, and the experience of referendums from around the world, be applied in London?

There are several different models.

Citizens of twenty-four US states and over 90 per cent of cities are allowed to collect signatures in favour of a particular proposition (usually a change to the law or to the delivery of services within a district).[257] Once a threshold number of signatories is passed, the motion is put to the vote. The result is binding in some cases, 'advisory' in others.

Citizens in Chicago voted on whether to ban firearms from restaurants (they voted yes), limit the size of gun magazines (yes again) and put up taxi fares (no!).[258] None were binding. These advisory referendums are seen as a useful way of gauging public opinion and engaging citizens in debate, but low turnouts weaken their validity: it's possible that a weighted opinion poll might be a better judge of opinion than the votes of a small, self-selected sample.

An alternative to the advisory initiative is the 'general policy initiative'. Here, citizens vote on the general thrust of a policy, which the legislature is then required to implement. This approach calls for arguments over the strength of a policy to be separated from debate over the detail of implementation. The Scottish referendum most closely resembled this approach.

The 'direct initiative' is another possibility. Here citizens vote directly on an amendment to existing legislation, so the law is implemented immediately if the voters are in favour. It yields little room for political manoeuvring but can lead to legislation that is incoherent or even contradictory.

A variant of this – practised most famously in Switzerland – is the 'indirect initiative'. Here initiatives with sufficient numbers of signatures are submitted first to the legislature (either the national government or the local Canton). They then have up to four years to deliberate and act on the measure before submitting it to the ballot. The legislature often takes action that satisfies those who submitted the petition and it is withdrawn. It is arguably less confrontational and more productive than a system that sees every successful petition sent straight to voters.

Even advisory ballots engage people in debate and gauge opinion in a way that City Hall usually struggles (or doesn't try) to achieve. Theoretically, anyone can gather enough signatures to trigger a ballot, forcing city leaders to tackle an issue that they might otherwise have overlooked. On the other hand, the process can be co-opted by vested interests and can become overwhelming if too many questions are being debated simultaneously. Many US cities and states limit the number of issues, but this then raises the question of how you decide which to pursue and which to drop.

We are persuaded by the case. We suggest that the next mayor should commit to a regular, annual ballot – the April Vote – thoroughly and independently evaluated over the four years of the next mayoral term.

Each year would see Londoners debate one general policy initiative related to areas over which the mayor has direct control, and one or two advisory initiatives on other issues, to engage public opinion on the major questions facing London whether or not they fall within the mayor's powers, to generate debate and strengthen the mayor's authority with government and others. Perhaps in the first year the questions could be chosen by the mayor and the GLA, but in subsequent years the public could submit propositions and those with the most signatures are automatically put to the vote.

The success of this approach to policy development in London couldn't be fairly assessed unless and until the referendum process is properly understood by voters and politicians. It needs the time to become embedded in a predictable cycle of discussion and decision. Over four years we would learn as much from the process as from the substance of the outcome.

This experimental ballot might also provide an opportunity to experiment with different forms of voting. London is rightly proud of its technological innovation, most recently in introducing world-leading contactless payment on the tube. Could we be among the pioneers here too? Might online voting encourage more participation, and could terminals in surprising places like supermarkets make it easier for new voters to join in? These new approaches could help to maximise participation in the April Vote and show the way for other elections.

## Establish a Citizens Budget

Citizen budgeting is a kind of referendum focused on an allocation of the budget. Here the mayor could earmark a fixed sum for spending on a range of possible initiatives. Citizens would be asked to choose between them. In Poznan, as we have seen, citizens have voted to fund a new shelter for homeless people, new bike lanes and the renovation of a sports complex.[90]

Parisians had the opportunity to choose between fifteen projects for a share of 5 per cent of the city's investment budget. Five million euros was up for grabs and citizens could vote online or in municipal polling stations. Options included 'learning gardens', mobile rubbish collection points, pop-up swimming pools, 'walls of vegetation' and play streets. Newly elected mayor Anne Hidalgo has promised that the people of the city will determine the destination at least €426 million (£335 million) before the end of her term and that they will be able to suggest their own ideas for subsequent ballots. Citizen budgeting is, she says, 'a new tool for citizens to participate, allowing all Parisians to propose and choose projects that will make the Paris of tomorrow. They will have real effect on local life. I see it as a major democratic innovation.'[259] So do we.

The Paris ballot has excited the interest of sections of the community who might not normally get excited about the democratic process. Media reports about young people campaigning for the swimming pool option show how a bold London mayor might reach parts of the electorate that might not otherwise be reached. We recommend a Citizens Budget for London – a serious allocation of the mayor's budget, a varied range of options and, in time, a process for engaging citizens in proposing ideas as well as well as in choosing between them. The referendum could take place as part of the April Vote each year, and the spending proposals could be for both pan-London investments and for specific local uses of the money.

## SOLVE PROBLEMS WITH OTHERS
### Build a 'London Table'

Developing shiny new ideas may be the best bit about being a mayor. Managing the disputes, tackling the seemingly intractable issues and dealing with crises is more testing. We think it is here that a new collaborative approach to leadership in the city is even more important.

In the first two weeks of Changing London six cyclists were killed in separate accidents across the city. Cycling fatalities weren't new but this sudden shocking spike in numbers stimulated debate and sparked a call for action. After a period of silence and uncertainty, and then an ill-judged comment that appeared to criticise the cyclists, Mayor Johnson reasserted the actions already underway to make the streets safer and pledged further endeavour.[260]

For a cycling mayor normally at ease with the media it was an uncharacteristically hesitant and vague performance that revealed a deeper weakness. He didn't know what to do but then, in truth, who would? The big city arteries, the neighbourhood high street and the residential crescents serve very different purposes but collectively they account for 80 per cent of our common, public space.[261] How do we share them? Who should use them, how should they use them and for what purpose? These questions are far too broad and multi-faceted for one person to answer but a robust response to multiple accidents on our roads needs a strategy that encompasses them all. Someone has to pull that together, and clearly that person should be the mayor.

Our correspondents ranged from the organised lobbies with well-rehearsed arguments and sophisticated research to individual Londoners with a particular personal experience. We discovered that there is no shortage of examples of how other cities have successfully promoted cycling. Groningen, for example – allegedly the most bike-friendly city in the world – divided itself into quarters and banned cars from travelling between them, pushing vehicles out onto the ringroad and clearing the roads for bikes.[201] In Copenhagen, 50 per cent of commuters travel by bike.[184] And every Sunday Bogotá closes 75 km of its roads to traffic, leaving them free for bikes, walkers and much else.[202]

Maybe none of this would work in London, but if ever there was an issue that cried out for collective wisdom, for learning from other cities and for pooling Londoners' ideas, then surely it is this.

In Sicily, Roberto Visentin, the mayor of Siracusa, has created the 'table for the future' – a multi-stakeholder organisation devoted first to building social cohesion and then to transforming Siracusa into 'a modern European city'.[262] The table facilitates collaboration on setting a shared vision and on identifying and managing projects where the goals are best achieved by pulling in the same direction.

A good mayor might use their unique position to convene a 'London Table' around the future of our streets. It would be a structured process expertly facilitated and designed to include and arbitrate between the views of key stakeholders, interested parties and private citizens.

A similar process could be adopted on other issues. Membership would change as the questions changed but the London Table should become a permanent part of the furniture of government. It should be expertly staffed, formally reporting to the London assembly, publicly accountable to the electorate and, like everything else in this chapter, judged on its ability to deliver a better future for the people of London.

## Convene a New Compact with Business

On almost all issues, the private sector would have an important role to play around the London Table. So important that we recommend the dedicated compact with business first proposed by Lucy Parker and Jon Miller on Changing London in January 2014:[263] 'Today's big companies are significant actors in society ... there is much in the record of business which is unacceptable, but it is also a powerful engine of progress and change... On our journey through the world of business we have found that some of the angriest fault lines in the relationship between business and society have become fertile ground for partnership.'

Politicians can struggle with finding the right approach to business. Attack dog or poodle? Too often it's one or the other. A period in which the square mile has so obviously pursued Mammon over principle may be a particularly testing time to start a more constructive conversation. And a mayor without a business to run and few powers over those that do run them may seem an odd person to start the talking. But if not now, then when? And if not our elected leader, then who?

Parker and Miller again: 'The next mayor should preside over the creation of a new social contract between business and society. That means opening up debate on some big questions.' They suggested several questions that might be on the agenda.

(1) In a city whose future success is so intricately connected to the behaviour of the City of London, how do we hold its leaders to their word when they say they want to earn back their standing as a centre for responsible banking?

(2) In a place where some people work for big businesses all week only to find they cannot afford to pay the rent, while others are incentivised beyond what was imaginable a generation ago, how do we establish a new consensus about what fairness looks like?

(3) When it's clear that public sector and private sector organisations both have a role to play in delivering the services that underpin lives and livelihoods in the city, how do we properly describe the best contribution each can make?

(4) And, looking to the city's sustainable, competitive position in the global economy, how do we build the skills and capacity necessary to make London a magnet for innovative businesses focused on developing products and services that respond to some of the greatest challenges facing the world today?

'It will take courage for the mayor to take this on and really work at establishing a serious and effective compact', concluded Parker and Miller. 'It's easier to go for attention-grabbing, vote-catching headlines which reinforce the polarisation between the worlds of business and politics. But to make London a city which is attractive as a place to live and work, and credible as a global city on the world stage, this is a conversation that the next mayor needs to initiate.'

## Lead Collaboration across the Public Sector

The London mayor has to work with government and with each of the London boroughs. Of course they must respect the responsibilities of others but they must also be sensitive to the needs of Londoners as a whole. They are, after all, our elected leader. Once again the 'mayoral super powers' – the voice, the visibility and the unique capacity to convene – can be particularly valuable.

The London Challenge, which drove up school standards in the capital, is an isolated but brilliant example of how collective action across the different tiers of government can yield dramatic and enduring change.[264] Similar collaboration is needed in other areas.

Matt Downie, for instance, wrote on Changing London about the issue of child abuse and neglect:[265] 'The prevalence and seriousness of the issue commands political attention across local and national government but so far not from either of the two London mayors. Why not?'

There are, Matt said:

good examples of local authorities working with their neighbours to pool resources and expertise, such as the 'Tri-Borough' arrangements in west London, and the leadership taken by Harrow in overseeing residential care for looked after children. However, these are the exceptions and in reality there are thirty-three separate systems for child protection in London, and an absence of strategic oversight.

Other cities offer examples of how a wider view of child protection can work. New York has its Blue Sky programme, backed by the city mayor, which co-ordinates programmes across a range of needs for children and young people. Closer to home, Manchester City Council works with the nine other councils across Greater Manchester to commission children's services.

How we care for children whose parents can't or don't is the defining characteristic of a civilised society. Strong leadership is essential at every level but it must be collaborative – poor communications and inadequate coordination are invariably cited in the most damaging case reviews. If the agencies serving London's children could raise school standards, why couldn't a similar collaborative effort enhance safeguarding, encourage reporting and actively promote fostering?

This doesn't need a hero in City Hall but it does need a collaborator – a mayor who is ready to use their powers of influence quietly and forcefully, delivering a better deal for London's most vulnerable citizens.

Child abuse and neglect is one set of issues in London, albeit a very important one. There are others that would benefit similarly, not from central direction but from far more effective collaboration. We need a mayor who will understand that great causes are the work of many hands and who will use their leadership to raise the banner, bang the drum and marshal the troops.

## INVOLVE LONDONERS IN DELIVERY AS WELL AS INVENTION

### Develop a London Calendar

Noting and acting on child abuse and neglect is the responsibility of every citizen. We need to be reminded, encouraged and emboldened over and over again. On this and many other issues, citizen engagement isn't a cheap alternative to statutory provision. It is an essential addition. Consider, for instance, health.

As we saw in the previous chapter, 140,000 people die every year in situations where their lives could have been saved if somebody had known first aid. Similar numbers, Frances Clarke pointed out, die from cancer. Not all the cancer deaths are avoidable but some are, and again basic knowledge and the confidence to act quickly are the keys to success.

Accidents happen and people get sick but avoiding the avoidable and taking swift action where we can seems like the most obvious common sense. It is all the more extraordinary, then, to learn from

132

Tahseen and Aisha Chowdhury[266] that one in five beds at the Royal London Hospital are occupied by patients with diabetes – a condition that, in many cases, could have been prevented entirely with lifestyle changes in earlier years.

Our contributors suggested several ways in which a good mayor might help tackle these issues. In almost every instance it is the barefoot solution, citizens helping themselves and helping others, rather than the professional provider, that makes the breakthrough. We can do this for ourselves but we need knowledge, very basic skills and a lot of encouragement.

We suggested in chapter five a Save Ourselves Week and suggested that making a date in this way focuses attention and is an approach that a good mayor might explore in relation to other themes. We've discussed, for instance, quite differently, work experience opportunities and, different again, opening up our great arts and cultural facilities for every child. In the second chapter we imagined that these and other ideas might be pulled together in a London Have-a-Go Festival, run over two weeks or even a month every year.

We suggest that a new London Calendar could be the organising framework. Creating moments with two or three such focal points every year provides a soap box for the mayor, and it provides us with the opportunity, the discipline, the excuse – the pressure even – to do the things we know we should but we've never quite got round to doing in the past, like thinking about the safety and well-being of the children down the road, checking for cancer or learning first aid.

## Create a Co-Production Academy

In Chapter 3 we discussed co-design and co-production and proposed the creation of a London Co-Production Academy to 'give Londoners the skills, confidence and opportunity to design and run the services that matter to them'. This kind of low-investment institution building could, in time, release a wave of change, influenced, perhaps inspired, by the mayor but neither owned nor directed by their office. It is an important way of sustaining the informed participation of service users and those around them, not only in imagining and planning the services they use but also in developing and delivering them together.

## WALK THE TALK

### Empower Cabinet Colleagues

Did you know that Barbara Windsor is the Mayor's ambassador for street parties? Yes, really, that Barbara Windsor.

Boris Johnson has seven deputy mayors and six mayoral advisers. An entirely unscientific survey led us to suspect that most Londoners would be unable to name or recognise any of them. There is also a coterie of eight special appointments; mostly people who are better known, but not for their work with the mayor: people like Barbara Windsor, Annie Lennox and Zandra Rhodes.[267]

In part this anonymity is a consequence of the dominant style of the current mayor. In part it is a consequence of a system that encourages the presidential approach. Either way a mayoralty that was better at involving the citizens of London would have more faces more prominently associated with its leadership. London needs a Brains Trust at the heart of its government, a team that brings together all the talents, and it needs a conventional, genuine, first-amongst-equals cabinet system with opportunities for colleagues to lead and, especially, to be seen to lead. This would do the job better and convey the right message. London is no longer a one-man show.

### And Recruit Them from Beyond the Political Pros

It's not for Changing London to comment on the merits of individual hopefuls, but we can't help but note that the first openly declared mayoral candidate, the journalist and policy expert Christian Wolmar, has not received the same attention from the media, let alone from Labour leaders, as parliamentary figures who are running. It is as if national parliamentary experience is considered to be an essential requirement for the role, but of course it isn't. Being a professional politician is not the only form of public service, or the only relevant apprenticeship. Indeed, some might argue that experience of life outside politics might be at least as useful in City Hall, if not more so. London is a city of many talents. Whoever does get the top job in 2016, they must draw colleagues from a gene pool wider than their own.

## Follow a Guiding Light

London needs a guiding light. At the start of this chapter we quoted the mayor of Mexico City López Obrador: 'For all and first for the poor.' A bias towards the poor has run through almost all our conversations on Changing London. It must, we think, be the pole star for the next London mayor. We think there is a moral argument for this position and also a political one.

A mayor who listened to and spoke for those whose voices are seldom heard and little understood could change this city. More than that, see how Boris Johnson has deployed the bully pulpit to plague the prime minister and become one of the UK's most recognisable politicians. Imagine how worthwhile that might have been if only he had had something to say that opened hearts and minds, that was constructive, healing, generous, collaborative, bold or inspiring. Speak here and be heard afar.

So-called minority issues don't, the pundits say, blow the dog whistle. Political fashion followers in wide-eyed thrall to the great American playbook would relegate many of the issues that we have prioritised on Changing London to, at best, second tier. Worthy, perhaps, of a ribbon cutting and a single speech but little more. This isn't merely another example of mayor de Blasio's 'lazy logic': it's just plain stupid. More Londoners experience mental illness than voted for Boris Johnson. More have either been sick themselves or cared for somebody who is than voted at all in the last mayoral election. Maybe not such a 'minority issue' after all?

Articulating a distinctive position on mental health may not in itself be sufficient to swing the next ballot, but maybe it could as one band of a rainbow alliance? 'An inclusive politics', says Jon Cruddas, 'is about building interests into coalitions for a common good.'[268]

This isn't an argument against the concept of a political party. As Elbaek and Lawson have written: 'someone has to stand the candidates, cohere the manifesto, set the budgets and establish the policy basis for letting go and platform building.'[269] But it is an argument for parties that move with the times. A same-old versus same-old contest in London in 2016 will not ignite the passions of an electorate that is young and substantially unaligned, identifies with issues not tribes, and is at best bored by politics as usual if not disaffected. A progressive platform, grounded in a bold and explicit set of values, connecting Londoners' everyday interests and built by us all, would offer new possibilities for the future of our city and for the future of our politics.

Look back at previous mayoral elections in London and consider the principal issues: fares, transport more generally, housing, planning. Important issues all. But then identify the dividing lines. On many the candidates have been arguing small differences. It is the point that President Obama made well on the campaign trail when he said: 'Challenging as they are, it's not the magnitude of our problems that concerns me the most, it's the smallness of our politics.'[270]

In the absence of distinction and a bigger politics, media discussion fixes on the marginal, and especially on trivia and personality. Is it any wonder that turnout at elections is low and getting lower?

Breaking out from the tramlines of the conventional discourse and talking about the issues that others never mention is difficult when the global economy or matters of war and peace are on the table. In national elections voters as well as candidates prefer the cautious and conventional, but city elections, as we've seen in numerous examples around the world, are not the same.

Here in the UK we have seen the electorate take a punt on independent candidates in the Police Commissioner elections and on mayors in Bristol and Middlesbrough. Even in London, both Livingstone and Johnson have found it helpful to put a certain distance between themselves and the Westminster mainstream.

Toes have been dipped, it's time for more.

## Last Words: Doing It for Ourselves

Over 6000 people slept rough in London last year.[271] That is a disgrace, and a challenge, and a good mayor would know that it matters even if the numbers involved – compared with the whole population – are relatively small.

Other faultlines in London involve much bigger numbers. The Centre for London's 'Hollow Promise' report focused on the 'Endies': the 20 per cent of Londoners who are low- to middle-income earners. Its authors concluded: 'while Endies don't complain they are increasingly disenchanted with the political system. Unless London does better by them, the city's politics could easily turn sour.'[272]

It is this combination of moral responsibility and political imperative that drives our determination to find new solutions and to help build a different kind of politics.

In one of the opening blogs on Changing London Steve Wyler quoted William Blake:[273]

> I wander thro' each charter'd street
> Near where the charter'd Thames does flow
> And mark in every face I meet
> Marks of weakness, marks of woe.

Steve pointed out that in linking the troubled faces with the repetition of the word 'chartered' Blake was connecting the sense of dispossession with the misery around him in the city. The city he observed did not belong to its citizens. It was, said Steve, 'owned by the powerful few, dominated by vested interests, controlled by the decrees of others, and sequestered from the people.' Subsequent contributors to Changing London painted a very similar picture of the city two hundred years later.

'There are no problems that we cannot solve together', Lyndon B. Johnson famously declared, 'and very few that we can solve by ourselves.'[274] London's faultlines in 2016 will not be best tackled by a few vested interests or by the random decrees of one man or woman.

Nor will they be most effectively and completely addressed by a mayor with only a list of things to do, no matter how useful those things might be. Gandhi's vivid phrase has been overworked to the brink of cliché but there is no better way of saying it: the next mayor must be the change we want to see in the world.

They must listen and collaborate, draw from the experience of the many, seek opinions on priorities, work with others on design and delivery, and root it all in a clear and unequivocal set of values consistently upheld.

We believe that a deeper democracy would be good for London in 2016.

We also think that a mayoral candidate offering this 'vote for values, deliver them together' approach to leadership would be smart politics.

London: a city led together. Governed by principles, made by us all.

# 7

## ANY QUESTIONS?

### WHAT'S THE BIG IDEA?

Books about politics usually have a unifying idea or ideology. The policies and particulars flow from that perspective. This one wasn't written like that. It is a collection of ideas from a lot of very different people. We've described Changing London as a warehouse of ideas but in pulling this rough guide together we realise that, though it has no pretensions to political sophistication and will never be taught on the PPE syllabuses of Oxbridge, there is an underlying, common-sense coherence to the various suggestions and a remarkable consistency of principle.

- Nine million people give the London mayor a big platform. We deserve an honest story teller with a good story – visionary, healing and just.
- Ideas abound in London and there is hope to harness. A smart mayor with an ear for common sense will embrace the optimism and the insight in the crowd and recognise that great causes are the work of many hands.
- Poverty casts a long shadow on this rich city. The capital is full of opportunities but they are unevenly distributed. A responsible steward won't shrink from the challenges of inequality.
- Quick fixes are tempting but sustainable solutions matter more. True leaders plant trees.
- Systems empower people but relationships change lives. A wise mayor will know that even in the greatest city it is the local bonds

and little bridges that make the places where we live. Attention to the individual, the specific, is not an alternative to a big vision: it is the making of it.

In these days of multiple parties, government coalitions and a febrile electorate, it is fashionable for our national leaders to talk of red lines – the ideological commitments that frame and define their politics, the non-negotiable. Here, flowing from the principles above and the preceding chapters, are some of ours.

**On communities:** one in four of our neighbours feel lonely often or all of the time. We shouldn't know that and yet do nothing, and in future we won't.

**On poverty:** a living wage is an entitlement in a rich city, not a privilege.

**On wealth:** remuneration distorted beyond the dreams of avarice is no more useful here and no more welcome than abject poverty.

**On housing:** houses in London are for people to live in. They should never be treated as investment vehicles.

**On transport:** vehicles service the city, our lifestyle depends on them, but ultimately people are more important than cars. In fact, people are more important than anything else.

**On politics:** only 38 per cent of those that were eligible voted in the 2012 mayoral election. This is a failure of politics and it is insane to do the same thing repeatedly and expect different results.

**On leadership:** a great city is not best served by a one-man show. London needs the kind of mayor that Maya Angelou had in mind when she said 'leaders see greatness in other people'.

And if we had to draw one word from all this that got closest to summarising it all, we think 'fairness' would be a strong contender but 'collaborative' is probably the one. Without a linguistic spin it may not be a vote clincher on the doorstep and no one will be marching down the Strand with placards for 'Collaboration now', but Changing London has been nothing but, and we think it is the future of politics in London.

The specifics – planning, designing and delivering in partnership with service users, 'tackling the faultlines' in a compact with business, cooperating across the sectors for a fitter, safer city and, even on the most contentious issues, building a London Table to resolve them together – are smart, common-sense ideas for 2016 and beyond. Good for London, good for politics and good for wannabe mayors.

We think collaboration is important at the very local level, with residents leading on the 'social acupuncture', the play streets and the Plotting Sheds; and we think it's important on the city-wide level, with Ideas for London and a London Fair Pay Commission. We even think it is important on the international stage, where the 'world's most collaborative city' would be an eye-catching counterpoint to the shallow bombast of the 'world's most competitive'. According to Wikipedia, London is twinned with eleven major world cities including Beijing, Paris, Bogotá, Moscow, Santiago and Tehran, but if that is true, you wouldn't know it from the GLA's website or, indeed, anywhere else we could find. Taking these relationships seriously would demonstrate London's leadership as an outward-looking, international steward, with an interest beyond national growth to promoting the well-being and development of the global community, not just its trading partners.

Caroline Middlecote wrote about some of the things that our next mayor might do to make this happen:[275]

> Reinvigorate the city 'twinning' system – cross the economic spectrum and move beyond the symbolic to building a meaningful relationship that will generate positive benefits for citizens of both nations.
>
> Promote international collaboration and social responsibility in enterprise: promote communication and exchange between start-ups in London and our twin cities, to catalyse new ideas and collaborations.
>
> Connect schools, universities, community events and groups.
>
> Promote exchanges between the GLA and local government with counterparts in our twin cities.
>
> Use communication with other countries as a way of promoting unity, respect and understanding within London.
>
> Demonstrate how this can be done successfully, to encourage other cities to build their own transformative friendships.

Caroline concludes: 'Being competitive alone can only take us so far; by being collaborative we can go much further. In the words of the African proverb – if you want to go fast, go alone. If you want to go far, go together.'

This is an attitude that could be equally profitably applied to London's place in the UK as well in the wider world. While 74 per cent of people living in the northwest of England think too many resources go to London,[276] the call for devolution of further powers will always be politically sensitive and the debate cries out for a more collaborative perspective.

As Ben Rogers has written, the case cannot be that 'London should get more money from Westminster but that London government can make better use of resources currently controlled from the centre … giving London more tax powers, in particular, will allow us to design a tax system that works for the capital and encourages growth, benefiting the country as a whole. But we accept that if London is to get more tax powers, it will get less central government grant.'[277]

Devolution to a collaborative capital is a good deal for Britain as well as a good deal for London but it mustn't stop there. Development specialists talk about the special challenges of the 'last mile' – the stage in the process when large-scale programmes reach the end user and are most likely to falter. The last mile for devolution takes the powers once exercised by Whitehall through regional and local government and then, most critically, out to community groups and individual citizens. It is on this final leg of the journey that ideas like Citizen Budgeting and the Co-Production Academy will have such an important part to play. In 2016, more than ever, London needs a mayor who is committed to collaborating, locally, nationally and globally.

## WHY DIDN'T YOU LOOK AT TRANSPORT, POLICING, PLANNING LAW, … ?

We offer this as nothing more than a rough guide to changing London: it's not a detailed roadmap. There will be any number of issues you will think we should have included. Good. The more ideas the better: we'd love to hear what we've missed, and more importantly the candidates must too.

We always aimed to be led by the contributions to Changing London and from them we picked out the five themes that spoke most loudly to us and, we hope, to other Londoners. Within those we rush headlong past vital issues that deserve entire books in themselves: housing policy, public transport, policing, education, childcare. Luckily, most of these big issues have seen books written about them and suffer no shortage of ideas. In particular, London's increasingly expensive, poor-quality and exploitative housing options seem set to dominate the next twelve months and even now have spawned a plethora of interesting ideas, passionately told.

There were other vital issues we fleetingly covered that receive less attention and deserve far more: child protection, domestic violence, mental health, illegally low pay. A good mayor would use their big platform to shout about these across the city.

And there are some crucial themes that didn't feature in our contributions and thus haven't appeared here at all. Most importantly, no city can plausibly laud itself as a success until the discrimination still endured by women and by London's large and diverse black and minority ethnic communities is wiped out for good.

But there was also one theme that prompted some excellent contributions, though not quite enough for a whole chapter. Since we started the book envisaging London as a great place to grow up, the final chapter seems a good place to briefly consider how we make London a great place to grow old.

From 2014, new housing developments in Vancouver have been required to install levers rather than knobs on doors and sinks. It might seem a bizarre intervention for city government, and for those in middle age or younger the choice is merely aesthetic. But for increasing numbers of us as we age and are more likely to develop arthritis, the doorknob is an unnecessary, sometimes crippling, hindrance to everyday life, when levers are so much easier to turn.

It is just one small example of the myriad ways in which being older or disabled is a barrier not because of age or disability itself but because of the way in which society around us has been designed or built.

Academics argue that cities should, in theory, be the best places to grow old.[278] Plenty of services, easy accessibility, dense living. But so far older people don't agree; we traditionally flee London for the coast as we age.

When the World Health Organisation looked at the age-friendliness of thirty-five major cities, they came up with a long and detailed, but ultimately simple, list of what makes our cities good for later life: it covered housing, transport, the design of buildings and outdoor space, the availability of community services, opportunities for civic participation and employment, and more. None of them trivial, but by no means insurmountable. The 'design' theme, for example, recommends 'a city that is clean; [with] well-maintained green spaces with adequate toilet facilities; pedestrian-friendly walkways; outdoor seating; smooth, well-maintained pavements; sufficient pedestrian crossings and street lighting.'[279] Hardly rocket science.

Yet London could do much better. Kate Jopling revealed how 10 per cent of those aged over 65 will be chronically lonely at any given time; today, at this moment, in London, that's around 94,000 people.[280] She said: 'Of course you cannot legislate for friendship, or write policies that require relationships, but the actions the next mayor takes have the power to enable or disable older people in keeping up the social contacts that are vital to their well-being. They have the power to value older people's contribution or to allow them to be cast aside; to ensure that statutory bodies take responsibility for supporting the social and emotional needs of the lonely individuals they encounter, or allow a continued focus on matters of life and limb only.'

What would help? Kate suggested some very practical changes: ensuring that public transport is accessible, and takes the right routes at the right times; pressuring the police to take older people's fear of crime seriously, particularly where it stops people leaving their house; and developing 'lifetime homes' for a full range of family situations. George Clarke suggested that the next mayor 'could start to make London the best city in the world for older people by leading a

Coffee and Chat; Tea and Talk drive to massively increase opportunities for older people to meet, chat and make friends.'[281] Clare Tickell called for better information for older people on available services, better community facilities, more opportunities to move into suitable housing, and a London-wide neighbourliness drive.[282] And Karl Brown suggested 'Elder Councils in each borough, possibly ... as Statutory Consultees, so lessons and experiences of the past are not lost on the present and future.'[283]

All these ideas and more would help ensure we continue to live happy, healthy, sociable lives well into older age. But that only scratches the surface of the possible. If we valued and sought to benefit from the accumulated wisdom of our elders, as some societies do but ours does not, we would improve the quality and even the length of our active lives and achieve positive outcomes for the wider community. We need to talk about how we harness this extraordinary resource in our institutions and our neighbourhoods. This is much more fundamental than a better-organised version of the disappointing Experience Corps or a rebranded iteration of the vacuous Big Society. A strong and purposeful vision needs funding and infrastructure, which Big Society never had, and it needs a bigger narrative and a wider debate than just another funding programme, but, if we are serious about making London a great place to grow old, we need to talk about a new social contract promising both security and comfort and real opportunities to contribute in our later years.

As James Beckles reminded us: 'London is a diverse and captivating global city but it is a city built upon its past as well as its future and those who have worked to make the capital what it is today should not be forgotten.'[284] Every 2016 candidate would do well to remember that baby boomers organise, influence and, above all, vote. The generation that swung London in the sixties can swing it again.

## Isn't It Unhelpful to Keep Banging on about the Rich and the Poor?

Many of the ideas in this guide are blind to income and class but some big ones are not. We have declared a sympathy for Mexico mayor López Obrador's approach – 'for all and first for the poor' – but also acknowledged that this kind of language wouldn't work in London. We have quoted the extensive evidence that supports the view that more-equal societies are good for everyone – healthier, happier and more successful – and we do not accept that it is 'the politics of envy' to point out that even big city institutions like Standard Life were affronted by the decision of Barclays to reward just 481 employees with bonuses worth £2.4 billion in 2014.[285] This kind of behaviour isn't good for London and it isn't even good for business. We put forward the idea of a Mayor's Share because we think these are the kinds of issue that progressive politicians ought to be talking about, at election time and while in office. If any further encouragement should be required, we say again that three-quarters of Londoners would support action to reduce the gap between high and low earners. Strong moral leadership can also be smart electoral politics.

## Isn't All This a Daydream?

Bright ideas are fine and dandy, the critics will say, but many of those here are beyond the powers of the mayor. We have three answers: stretch the super powers, get more and are you sure?

### Stretch the Super Powers

We covered this in Chapter 1 but, to briefly repeat what was said there, the great change-making mayors across the world achieve extraordinary things not only, or even primarily, through the exercise of their formal powers but through the powers of influence. The London mayor has high visibility: barely a day goes by when Londoners don't read about Boris Johnson in the evening paper or see him on the regional news. His voice is heard in the sitting rooms of Londoners and in the boardrooms of our decision makers. Backed by the UK's biggest directly elected mandate this exceptional prominence confers a unique capacity to convene. The mayoral super powers have been underused in London. It's time to stretch them.

**Get More**

As we've noted above, devolution is in the wind. It will be a theme of the next mayoralty whoever wins office. There is a very simple answer for the mayor that doesn't have the powers that they need to meet the needs of Londoners: get more. Or at least be an activist mayor and campaign for them.

**Are You Sure?**

We don't mean to patronise, but when local agencies in the US were invited to seek rule changes or new freedoms under the provisions of an Urban Enterprise Zone, many were surprised to discover that they already had the levers they needed, they just never used them. Apparently, the experience of the Total Place authorities in the UK has been similar. Big bureaucracies operate as much on custom and practice as they do by the rulebook. Politics is the art of the possible, and the possible could well be more than has ever been done before.

## Is This Just about the Labour Party?

It is true that we declared a focus on 'Labour' mayoral candidates at the outset but the discussion on the blog hasn't been partisan and almost all the great exemplars from elsewhere are similarly resistant to easy classification. We, the authors of this book and curators of the site, haven't exercised any political censorship on content and, of course, by its very nature, the Changing London website is open to everybody; policy ideas normally hatched in Westminster cubby holes are germinating here in the clear light of day. And what if candidates from other parties picked them up? An election based on great ideas? Wouldn't that be wonderful?

However, we have thought it important to lead this debate with absolute transparency. Politicians contaminate democracy with too much nuance and duplicity, second guessing when the big issues demand an urgent honesty. Elections are political and politics is about governing, about choices and who should take them, and especially about the ideological foundations on which those decisions will be based. A greater equality is at the heart of our vision for the world and for London. We are under no illusions about the Labour Party but we think it is, in the end, the vehicle most likely to take us closest to that ultimate goal.

The best faith-based charities work with everyone who needs them and everyone who shares their humanitarian objectives, but they are also straightforward about where they come from. A political movement is different, but there is an example here for politics: clear and explicit values underpinning big broad collaborative programmes.

We think that this approach is morally correct and also pragmatic – a combination that may account for the encouraging level of attention that Changing London has received so far from actual and possible candidates.

All this opens up the possibility that, if Changing London is rooted in a progressive view of the world, it might be possible and similarly pragmatic for others to run a similar exercise from a different perspective. Of course we are biased, and it might be possible, but we think it is unlikely. It is hard for us to imagine a book like this – bursting with strong, creative ideas – growing from the arid soils of a UKIP ideology.

## MIGHT THE PROCESS WORK ON A NATIONAL SCALE?

As we explained in Chapter 1, cities are different from smaller municipalities and from nation states. That's why we think they are, potentially, such exciting places for developing new ideas. Crowdsourcing ideas for the defence of the realm would be a very different exercise from imagining a city of play streets and citizen budgets. However, the really big idea here is less in the specifics and more in the underpinning principle – the idea that voters may have the will, and certainly have the capacity, to contribute far more to the democratic process than a cross in a box once every four or five years. Capturing that potential may yet save politics from a dystopian future characterised by shrinking parties, unpopular leaders, ineffectual coalitions and an electorate that is either distrusting, disinterested or most probably both. Of course a simple blog and a little book won't reverse the direction of travel but we do hope it might signal the need for, and the potential of, a different approach.

The big parties, who most need to listen, may be the last to hear. Big organisations are difficult to change but 'open network parties' are rapidly becoming an intriguing and disruptive feature in other democracies across the world.

'Five Star in Italy prides itself on its internet-based decision making structure, as do the Pirate Parties in Iceland, Germany and Sweden', writes Geoff Mulgan. 'Democracy OS in Argentina has designed a sophisticated way for all its members to propose ideas and shape them online and Podemos in Spain is rapidly emerging as one of Europe's most impressive parties, combining mass public support, serious policy prescriptions (the *Financial Times* recently praised them for having one of the most coherent approaches to post-crisis economic management), and, again, a radical use of the internet to involve supporters.'[286]

With all the energy and excitement of the insurgent and none of the baggage that burdens the incumbent, these crowdsourced politicians have the well-tuned antennae and the nimble creativity that the established parties so visibly lack.

In the 2013 Australian Federal election, community campaigners in the traditionally safe seat of Indi built an effective movement for change largely through the use of social media and fronted by independent candidate Cath McGowan. 'Indi', said Campbell Klose and Nick Haines, 'had never seen anything like it. For the first time in living memory thousands of people from all walks of life were engaging in politics and having a say in how they would like to see their electorate represented. For too long they had been taken for granted.'[287] McGowan won the seat.

At a local level, if not yet at a national one, the warning for the big beasts in the UK is very clear: a different kind of politics is on the way. Adapt or be beaten.

# Why the Focus on the Primaries in 2015? Surely the Mayoral Election in 2016 is the Main Event?

Both matter but we think that the run up to the selection of the candidate is a critical time for sharing new ideas. When candidates are selected and the mayoral election starts in earnest, the manifestos will be firming up. Our best chance of generating a debate and beginning to influence mayoral programmes will be during the primary campaigns (May, June, July), when it will be necessary for all the candidates to identify some points of difference in a crowded field.

## Who Is Your Favourite Candidate?

We don't have one and, with all due respect, nor should you, not until we've all seen the substance of the policies on offer.

## What Should I Do Now?

**Carry on imagining:** you will know what needs to change in London. It may be sparked by an idea in this book, or something you spotted yesterday, or it could be a plot you've been hatching for a while. Share your ideas on Changing London (www.change-london.org.uk) and read what others have come up with too.

**Be heard at a hustings:** for the primary campaigns in summer 2015 and the election itself in spring 2016. Push the candidates and stretch them with the breadth of your vision for London and the standards you expect of our next mayor. Share the ideas in the book or ideas of your own.

**Do it yourself:** London isn't made by the mayor alone – anything but. Many of the ideas in the book could be made real in your neighbourhood, right now. Pick something and have a go – set up a play street or a community group, campaign for local businesses to pay the living wage or, if you run a business yourself, start paying it. Join something, start something. Do something.

**Hold the winner to their word:** twenty-first-century politics is synonymous with broken promises, but if London's next mayor is going to be different, they must start by sticking to their word. It is our job to make sure they do.

**Keep it up:** ideas can take time to germinate and even a superhero mayor won't be able to do everything in their first year. Persevere.

# Last Words

We have two final words of advice for London's new leader.

When the Scottish Parliament was opened in 2004, the words of Canadian poet Dennis Lee were paraphrased by Alasdair Gray and inscribed on the Canongate wall: 'Work as if you live in the early days of a better nation'.

For every generation there are those 'early days'. Full of hope and opportunity. Our city will have new leadership in May 2016 and the new mayor will very likely have new powers to sit alongside the existing ones, particularly the mayoral super powers that have been too seldom applied for the common good.

It will be spring time in the capital and time for changing London.

*Be bold.*

# Endnotes

1. Cruddas, J., and Rutherford, J. (2014), *One Nation: Labour's Political Renewal*. London: One Nation Register.

2. Turnout was 38 per cent in the 2012 mayoral election. Data from Electoral Commission (2012), Greater London Authority elections 2012: report on the administration of the elections held on 3 May 2012.

3. Two were controlled by the Liberal Democrats and two were under no overall control. Data from London Councils. See www.londoncouncils.gov.uk/londonfacts/elections2014/2010.htm#.VNP-WSVWsVfw [accessed February 2015].

4. BBC (2012), Lonely London: poll suggests a quarter feel alone. *BBC News*, 20 November. Available at www.bbc.co.uk/news/uk-england-london-20324373 [accessed February 2015].

5. In 2014 child poverty in London was measured at 37 per cent according to the London Poverty Profile. See www.londonspovertyprofile.org.uk/ [accessed January 2015].

6. Cecil, N. (2014), Rich Londoners live 25 years longer than people from poorer parts of the capital. *Evening Standard*, 14 January.

7. Katz, B., and Bradley, J. (2013), *The Metropolitan Revolution: How Cities and Metros are Fixing Our Broken Politics and Fragile Economy*. Brookings Institution Press.

8. Johnson, C. (2014), Sharing City Seoul, a model for the world. Available at www.shareable.net/blog/sharing-city-seoul-a-model-for-the-world [accessed February 2015].

9. National League of Cities (2012), Educational alignment for young children: profiles of local innovation.

10. Stockholm Vision 2030: a guide to the future. Available at http://international.stockholm.se/globalassets/ovriga-bilder-och-filer/framtidsguiden_eng.pdf [accessed February 2015].

11. PRI.org (2009), Amsterdam climate neutral by 2025. Available at www.pri.org/stories/2009-07-10/amsterdam-climate-neutral-2025 [accessed February 2015].

12. De Blasio, B. (2014), Bill de Blasio's speech to the Labour conference (full text). Available at www.newstatesman.com/politics/2014/09/bill-de-blasios-speech-labour-conference-full-text [accessed January 2015].

13. Leach, A. (2014), Why the tattooed mayor of Thessaloniki is a beacon of hope for Greece. *The Guardian*, 30 December.

14. Toro, F. (2014), Keep calm and Nenshi on: how floods turned the Calgary mayor into a folk hero. *The Guardian*, 30 December.

15. City Mayors Foundation. Available at www.citymayors.com/gratis/city_mayors.html [accessed February 2015.]

16. See, for example, Berardino, M. (2012), Mike Tyson explains one of his most famous quotes. *Sun Sentinel*, 9 November.

17. Pearce, N. (2014), Painting in primary colours: political populism and the muted mainstream. IPPR Blog, 11 November. Available at www.ippr.org/nicks-blog/ [accessed February 2015].

18. Ipsos Mori (2013), Politicians trusted less than estate agents, bankers and journalists. Available at www.ipsos-mori.com [accessed February 2015].

19. Dudman, J. (2014), Devo Manc: what powers will the new Greater Manchester Mayor have? *The Guardian*, 3 November.

20. PWC (2014), Cities of opportunity 2014. Available at www.pwc.com/us/en/cities-of-opportunity/index.jhtml [accessed January 2015].

21. Unpublished quantitative analysis of BritainThinks 2014 'Capital Gains?' research, used with kind permission. Available on request.

22. From 'Choruses from the Rocks', published as part of T. S. Eliot's *Collected Poems*.

23. In 2014 child poverty in London was measured at 37 per cent according to the London Poverty Profile. See www.londonspovertyprofile.org.uk/ [accessed January 2015].

24. Yougov survey reported in Dave Hill's London blog: 'Guess what? Most Londoners think London is good – especially for the young'. *The Guardian*, 19 March.

25. Quoted in Ives, S. (2004), The politics of happiness. *Yes! Magazine*, 20 May. Available at www.yesmagazine.org/issues/finding-courage/the-politics-of-happiness [accessed January 2015].

26. Documentary available in Goodyear, S. (2013), How a few Dutch children fought for a street where they could play, and won. *Citylab*, 12 December. Available at www.citylab.com/commute/2013/12/how-few-dutch-children-fought-street-where-they-could-play-and-won/7855/ [accessed January 2015].

27. Duffin, C. (2014), Streets are alive with the sound of children playing. *Daily Telegraph*, 22 February. Available at www.telegraph. co.uk/health/children_shealth/10654330/Streets-are-alive-with-the-sound-of-children-playing.html [accessed January 2015].

28. TfL (2013), The vision and direction for London's streets and roads. London Roads Task Force.

29. Appleyard, D. (1981), *Liveable Streets*. Berkeley, CA: University of California Press.

30. Hochschild, T. R. (2013), The cul-de-sac effect: relationship between street design and residential social cohesion. *Journal of Urban Planning and Development* 141(1), 05014006.

31. Sampson, R. (2013), When disaster strikes, it's survival of the sociable. *New Scientist* 2916 (May).

32. See http://playingout.net and www.londonplay.org.uk/.

33. City of Rotterdam (2010), Rotterdam, city with a future: how to build a child friendly city. Available at www.rotterdam.nl/JOS/kindvriendelijk/Rotterdam%20City%20with%20a%20future.pdf [accessed January 2015].

34. Lawson, N. (2012), Ban outdoor advertising. *The Guardian*, 20 April. Amusing Planet (2013), São Paulo: the city with no outdoor advertisements. Available at www.amusingplanet.com/2013/07/sao-paulo-city-with-no-outdoor.html [accessed January 2015].

35. See www.lemonde.fr/societe/article/2014/11/24/grenoble-commence-a-bannir-la-publicite-de-ses-rues_4528080_3224.html.

36. Bunting, C. (2013), Cultural engagement by young Londoners: an introduction to key trends, drivers and challenges. A New Direction.

37. Bristol City Council: make Sunday special. Available at www.bristol.gov.uk/page/leisure-and-culture/make-sunday-special [accessed January 2015].

38. See http://kidsinmuseums.org.uk/takeoverday/ [accessed February 2015].

39. Innovation Unit/A New Direction (2012), Inspirational cultural programmes. A New Direction.

40. Violi, C. (2014), Brokerage models a horizon scan. A New Direction.

41. McKenzie, B. (2014), Greenwich blog. A New Direction. Available at www.anewdirection.org.uk/blog/partnerships-for-place-and-people [accessed February 2015].

42. Jovchelovitch, S., and Concha, N. (2013), Kids company: a diagnosis of the organisation and its interventions. Report, London School of Economics.

43. Ofsted (2010), London challenge. Available at http://webarchive.nationalarchives.gov.uk/20141124154759/www.ofsted.gov.uk/sites/default/files/documents/surveys-and-good-practice/l/London%20Challenge.pdf [accessed January 2015].

44. Save the Children (2012), Developing children's zones for England. Available at www.savethechildren.org.uk/sites/default/files/docs/Developing-Childrens-Zones-summary.pdf [accessed January 2015].

45. National League of Cities (2012), Educational alignment for young children: profiles of local innovation.

46. SA2020: what is SA2020? Available at www.sa2020.org/sa2020-history/ [accessed January 2015].

47. Kania, J., and Cramer, M. (2011), Collective impact. *Stanford Social Innovation Review* 6 (21 January).

48. See www.standard.co.uk/news/get-london-reading/.

49. Community Links and Brown (2007), *Britain's Everyday Heroes: The Making of the Good Society.* Mainstream Publishing.

50. See www.readongeton.org.uk/.

51. Fostering Network (2014), Thousands of new foster families needed in 2014. Available at https://www.fostering.net/media/2014/thousands-new-foster-families-needed-in-2014#.VLfzhYqsVfy [accessed January 2015].

52. New Policy Institute/Trust for London (2013), London's poverty profile 2013.

53. See www.internaware.org/.

54. London Poverty Profile: www.londonspovertyprofile.org.uk/ [accessed January 2015].

55. Bell, K. (2013), Investing in childhood. *Fabian Review.* Available at www.fabians.org.uk/investing-in-childhood/ [accessed January 2015].

56. Williams, Z. (2010), It is disheartening and short-sighted to abandon this incentive to save. *The Guardian,* 25 May. Available at www.theguardian.com/money/2010/may/25/child-trust-funds-zoe-williams [accessed January 2015].

57. Kleiman, N., Forman, A., Ko, J., Giles, D., and Bowles, J. (2013), Innovation and the city. Centre for an Urban Future.

58. *Daily Telegraph* (2013), Childcare costs are like a second mortgage (6 March).

59. Bell, K. (2013), Childcare and maternal employment in London. Child Poverty Action Group.

60. Shorthouse, R., Masters, J., and Mulheirn, I. (2012), A better beginning: easing the cost of childcare. Social Market Foundation.

61. Greater London Authority (2014), A fairer London: the 2014 living wage in London.

62. Mayor of London (2013), The mayor's housing covenant: making the private rented sector work for London.

63. Action for Children (2014), Paying the price: can we help the most vulnerable young people avoid unmanageable debt?

64. Bowyer (2013), Pedal power is top priority for new Leeds children's mayor. *Yorkshire Evening Post*, 13 November.

65. Quoted at www.goodreads.com [accessed January 2015].

66. Brook, K. (2005), Labour market participation: the influence of social capital. Office for National Statistics/Labour Market Trends.

67. Victor, C. R., and Bowling, A. (2012), Longitudinal analysis of loneliness among older people in Great Britain. *Journal of Psychology* 146(3), 313–31.

68. Gilbert, K., Quinn, S., Goodman, R., Butler, J., and Wallace, J. (2013), A meta-analysis of social capital and health: a case for needed research.5 *Journal of Health Psychology* 18(11), 1385–99.

69. Changing London, 27 November 2013.

70. Quoted at the London Conference 2013. See also a similar quote in Luce, E. (2014), Rahm Emanuel: Mayor America. *Financial Times*, 14 February.

71. Quoted in McGregor, J. (2014), Maya Angelou on leadership, courage and the creative process. *Washington Post*, 28 May.

72. Changing London, 12 November 2013.

73. Changing London, 19 March 2014.

74. See http://brixtonpound.org/ [accessed January 2015].

75. See http://myhigh.st/ [accessed January 2015]

76. Changing London, 4 December 2013.

77. Links to each initiative and more information available in Tessy's post at www.change-london.org.uk.

78. Community Links (2008), Side by side: a report setting out the Council on Social Action's work on one-to-one.

79. Changing London, 18 December 2013.

80. Changing London, 22 November 2013.

81. Carr-West, J., and Wilkes, L. (2013), The big lunch: feeding community spirit. Local Government Information Unit.

82. Changing London, 29 November 2013.

83. Changing London, 20 December 2013.

84. Changing London, 6 December 2013.

85. Kaye, L. (2011), Could cities' problems be solved by urban acupuncture? *The Guardian*, 21 July.

86. Greater London Authority (2014), London mental health: the invisible costs of mental ill health.

87. Derived using data from TfL (January 2015).

88. Changing London, 24 March 2014.

89. Changing London, 18 March 2014.

90. Brefort, L. (2013), If Vienna and Poznan can do it, so can Belgrade and others. World Bank. Available at www.worldbank.org/en/news/opinion/2013/06/04/if-vienna-and-poznan-can-do-it-so-can-belgrade-and-others [accessed January 2015].

91. Changing London, 16 April 2014.

92. See http://bcnopenchallenge.org/ [accessed January 2015].

93. Leadbeater, C., and Garber, J. (2010), *Dying for Change*. London: Demos.

94. From work by the LGA led by Stephen Jacobs. For example, see thepresentation at http://s3-eu-west-1.amazonaws.com/doc.housing.org.uk/B3_-_Stephen_Jacobs__Gwyn_Owen.pdf [accessed January 2015].

95. See www.blood.co.uk/about-blood/ [accessed January 2015].

96. Changing London, 21 January 2014.

97. Caballero, M. (2004), Academic turns city into a social experiment. *Harvard University Gazette*. Available at http://news.harvard.edu/gazette/2004/03.11/01-mockus.html [accessed January 2015].

98. Quoted in Richardson, R. (2000), Stories and policies. Runnymede Trust. Available at www.runnymedetrust.org/uploads/projects/meb/bgPoliciesAndStories.html [accessed January 2015].

99. Nelson, L., and Norton, M. (2004), From student to superhero: situational primes shape future helping. *Journal of Experimental Psychology* 41, 423–30.

100. Changing London, 11 December 2013.

101. Changing London, 9 December 2013.

102. See http://sfcontroller.org/index.aspx?page=405 [accessed January 2015].

103. See www.nyc.gov/html/planyc2030/html/theplan/introduction.shtml [accessed January 2015].

104. Kennedy, R. (1968), Remarks at the University of Kansas (18 March). Available at JFK library website: www.jfklibrary.org [accessed January 2015].

105. Changing London, 12 November 2013.

106. Changing London, 20 November 2013.

107. Quoted at www.un.org/en/globalissues/briefingpapers/humanrights/quotes.shtml [accessed January 2015].

108. London's GVA (similar to GDP) was equivalent to $760 billion in 2013 (ONS, Regional Gross Value Added, December 2013 release). The UK's GDP in 2013 was $2.7 trillion and Switzerland's was $685 billion (World Bank, data.worldbank.org [accessed January 2015]).

109. High Pay Centre (2015), Fatcat Tuesday: executive pay has already overtaken your earnings for the entire year. Available at http://highpaycentre.org/ [accessed January 2015].

110. Leach, A. (2014), Your house earns more than you. *Daily Mirror*, 21 August.

111. London Poverty Profile (2014), Low pay risk by hours. Available at www.londonspovertyprofile.org.uk/indicators/topics/low-pay/low-pay-risk-by-hours/index.html [accessed January 2015].

112. Survation (2014), Online polling of London residents on behalf of the London Child Poverty Alliance. Available at http://survation.com/wp-content/uploads/2014/04/London-Residents-Poll-Report.pdf [accessed January 2015].

113. Tawney, R. H. (1913), Poverty as an industrial problem. Inaugural Lecture. Reproduced in *Memoranda on the Problems of Poverty* (London: William Morris Press).

114. Treanor, J., and Farrell, S. (2014), UK only G7 country with wider inequality than at turn of century. *The Guardian*, 14 October.

115. Barbaro, M., and Chen, D. (2013), De Blasio is elected New York City mayor in landslide. *New York Times*, 5 November.

116. Lanning, T., and Lawton, K. (2011), Getting what we deserve: attitudes to pay, reward and desert. Interim Report, IPPR.

117. Stewart, H. (2013), Reading tops list of 'good growth' towns and cities in the UK. *The Guardian*, 18 November.

118. London Poverty Profile: www.londonspovertyprofile.org.uk/ [accessed January 2015].

119. Left Foot Forward (2014), Number of Londoners using foodbanks doubles, new figures show. *Left Foot Forward*, 10 June.

120. Lupton, R. (2013), A tale of two cities? LSE British Politics and Policy blog, 2 October. Available at http://blogs.lse.ac.uk/politicsandpolicy/a-tale-of-two-cities/ [accessed January 2015].

121. Changing London, 17 December 2013.

122. Florida, R. (2014), A $10.10 minimum wage would affect some metros much more than others. *Citylab*, 29 January.

123. Hutton, W. (2014), Minimum wage: Seattle proves that the fight for decent pay can and must be won. *Observer*, 7 June.

124. Changing London, 5 February 2014.

125. Wales, R. (2014), Newham mayor Sir Robin Wales is cracking down on poverty pay. *Newham Recorder*, 26 February.

126. London Assembly Economy Committee (2014), Fair pay: making the London living wage the norm. GLA.

127. Greater London Authority (2014), A fairer London: the 2014 living wage in London.

128. Matheson, G. (2014), Speech by Councillor Gordon Matheson (21 November). Available at https://www.glasgow.gov.uk/index.aspx?articleid=14387 [accessed January 2015].

129. *Huffington Post* (2014), NYC mayor wants corporate welfare queens to pay a living wage. *Huffington Post*, 2 March.

130. Chakrabortty, A. (2014), Poverty pay isn't inevitable. Look to the cleaners of New York. *The Guardian*, 8 September.

131. Dillow, C. (2014), Unions and productivity. Stumbling and mumbling. Available at http://stumblingandmumbling.typepad.com/stumbling_and_mumbling/2014/07/unions-productivity-.html [accessed January 2015].

132. Hughes, C., and Crowley, L. (2014), London: a tale of two Cities. The Work Foundation, London.

133. Changing London, 17 February 2014.

134. Berube, A. (2013), How mayors can grapple with inequality. Brookings Institute blog, 5 December. Available at www.brookings.edu/blogs/the-avenue/posts/2013/12/05-mayors-inequality-berube [accessed January 2015].

135. Changing London, 22 January 2014.

136. London Finance Commission (2013), Raising the capital: the report of the London Finance Commission.

137. Goldsmith, S. (undated), City Hall and religion: when, why and how to lead. Harvard University, Kennedy School of Government.

138. Pensions Policy Institute (2011), The implications of government policy for future levels of pensioner poverty.

139. Changing London, 6 January 2014.

140. Kirkup, J. (2014), Labour has no problem with people making 'a lot of money'. *Daily Telegraph*, 2 May.

141. The Equality Trust (2014), A divided Britain: inequality within and between the regions.

142. TUC (2014), Pay inequality has soared across London and the South East since 2000. Available at www.tuc.org.uk/economic-issu es/britain-needs-pay-rise/pay-inequality-has-soared-across-lond on-and-south-east-2000 [accessed January 2015].

143. Kollewe, J. (2014), London retains crown as favourite city of world's ultra-rich. *The Guardian*, 5 March.

144. Riddell, M., and Ross, T. (2013), Rachel Reeves interview: 'minimum wage would be £19 an hour if it rose like bosses' pay'. *Daily Telegraph*, 20 September.

145. Johnson, B. (2013), Boris Johnson's speech at the Margaret Thatcher lecture (in full). *Daily Telegraph*, 28 November.

146. Changing London, 10 February 2014.

147. Wilkinson, R., and Pickett, K. (2010), The impact of income inequality on sustainable development in London. London Sustainable Development Commission.

148. Changing London, 14 April 2014.

149. From Hutton, W. (2001), The rich aren't cleverer, just richer. *The Guardian*, 1 April.

150. De Blasio, B. (2014), Text of Bill de Blasio's first State of the City address (10 February).

151. Transport for London (2014). Annual report and statement of accounts 2013/14.

152. Bosteels, K. (2014), Record turnover and profit for Burberry. *Retail Detail*, 22 May.

153. High Pay Centre (2014), Reform agenda: how to make top pay fairer.

154. Hutton, W. (2011), Hutton review of fair pay in the public sector: final report.

155. Adam, S., and Browne, J. (2012), Reforming Council Tax Benefit. IFS Commentary C123.

156. Tuhus-Dubrow, R. (2010), Surprising potential of voluntary taxes. *Dallas Morning News*, 20 August.

157. Changing London, 10 February 2014.

158. Patton, Z. (2012), The boss of Boston: Mayor Thomas Menino. *Governing*, January.

159. OECD (2014), Focus on inequality and growth: December 2014.

160. Share Action (2014), The case for the living wage: why a living wage pays dividends.

161. ONS (2014), Public sector employment Q1 2014.

162. Changing London, 12 February 2014.

163. Rogers, B. (2014), An alternative to a Tourist Tax – a T-Bid. Centre for London blog (4 June).

164. Hodgkinson, T. (2014), Campaigners call for 30-hour working week to allow for healthier, fairer society – and more time for fun. *Independent*, 24 April.

165. Cecil, N. (2014), Housing crisis overtakes transport as biggest concern for Londoners, poll suggests. *Evening Standard*, 15 April.

166. Hill, D. (2013), London housing crisis: a tax on speculators? *The Guardian*. 1 October.

167. Cumming, E. (2013), Is there any hope for first time buyers? *Daily Telegraph*, 1 February.

168. Mayor of London (2013), The mayor's housing covenant: making the private rented sector work for London.

169. Boffey, D. (2014), Private landlords cash in on right-to-buy – and send rents soaring for poorest tenants. *The Guardian*, 12 January.

170. *The Economist* (2013), The parasitic city. *The Economist,* 3 June.

171. Wood, J. (2013), Overseas occupiers at Stratford Plaza. *East Magazine*, 8 March.

172. Westcott, L. (2014), Bill de Blasio seeks to end New York City's 'poor doors'. *Newsweek*, 23 July.

173. Hill, D. (2014), Outraged by 'poor doors'? See how you like the alternatives. *The Guardian*, 28 July.

174. London Assembly (2014), Assembly highlights weaknesses in Mayor's housing strategy (2 April).

175. Changing London, 12 December 2014.

176. Changing London, 8 January 2014.

177. Changing London, 17 June 2014.

178. O'Sullivan, F. (2014), Paris wants to keep central neighborhoods from becoming 'ghettos for the rich'. *Citylab*, 19 December.

179. O'Sullivan, F. (2013), Has Germany figured out the way to keep rents affordable? *Citylab*, 20 November.

180. Oh, I. (2014), This is what Bill De Blasio has done for New York City in his first 6 months. *Huffington Post*, 7 January.

181. Badger, E. (2014), New York state floats a tax credit for renters. *Citylab*, 7 January.

182. Govan, F. (2012), Spanish mayor hailed as modern-day Robin Hood. *Daily Telegraph*, 10 August.

183. Daunton, M. (2004), London's 'great stink' and Victorian urban planning. *BBC History*. Available at www.bbc.co.uk/history/trail/victorian_britain/social_conditions/victorian_urban_planning_04.shtml [accessed January 2015].

184. London Health Commission (2014), Better health for London: the report of the London Health Commission. GLA. Available at www.londonhealthcommission.org.uk [accessed January 2015].

185. Bunker, J. (2001), The role of medical care in contributing to health improvements within societies. *International Journal of Epidemiology* 30(6), 1260–63.

186. Durkin, E. (2013), Mayor Bloomberg put saving lives first as he embarked on public health crusades. *New York Daily News*, 19 December.

187. Derived from http://life.mappinglondon.co.uk/# [accessed January 2015].

188. Guatemala life expectancy obtained from *CIA World Factbook*. See www.cia.gov/library/publications/the-world-factbook/rankorder/2102rank.html [accessed January 2015].

189. Changing London, 14 April 2014.

190. Wilkinson, R., and Pickett, K. (2010), *The Spirit Level: Why Equality is Better for Everyone*. Penguin.

191. Pickett, K. (2014), Addressing health inequalities through greater social equality at a local level: implement a living wage policy. In 'If you could do one thing... Nine local actions to reduce health inequalities' (British Academy).

192. Changing London, 17 February 2014.

193. John Hopkins Sheridan Libraries: the Hippocratic oath (modern version). Available at http://guides.library.jhu.edu/content.php?pid=23699&sid=190964 [accessed January 2015].

194. Leadbeater, C. (2014), The London recipe: how systems and empathy make the city. Centre for London.

195. Holt-Lunstad, J., Smith, T., and Layton, J. (2010), Social relationships and mortality risk: a meta-analytic review. *PLoS Med* 7(7), e1000316.

196. Changing London, 10 December 2013.

197. Clark, A. (2004), Want to feel less stress? Become a fighter pilot not a commuter. *The Guardian*, 20 November.

198. Transport for London (2012), London streets factsheet. Available at http://tfl.gov.uk/cdn/static/cms/documents/london-streets-factsheet.pdf [accessed January 2015].

199. Transport for London (2012), Attitudes towards cycling annual report 2012. Available at www.tfl.gov.uk/cdn/static/cms/documents/attitudes-towards-cycling-2012-report.pdf [accessed January 2015].

200. Transport for London (2012), Attitudes to walking 2012: research summary. Available at www.tfl.gov.uk/cdn/static/cms/documents/attitudes-to-walking-2012-summary.pdf [accessed January 2015].

201. Goodyear, S. (2013), The city where bicycles rule the road. *Citylab*, 10 October.

202. Power, M. (2010), Bogotá's Ciclovia could teach Boris Johnson how to run a car-free capital. *The Guardian*, 16 June.

203. BBC News (2013), Traffic-free shopping day in London's West End scrapped (11 October). Available at www.bbc.co.uk/news/uk-england-london-24499194 [accessed January 2015].

204. London Green Party (2014), Mayor will spend up to 28 times more on road building than on cycling infrastructure (18 November).

205. Changing London, 10 December 2013.

206. Changing London, 8 April 2015.

207. Vidal, J. (2013), London told to cut air pollution by 2020 – or face fines. *The Guardian*, 18 December.

208. Mathieson, K. (2014), Why license plate bans don't cut smog. *The Guardian*, 20 March

209. Duggan, J. (2014), Beijing to spend £76bn to improve city's air quality. *The Guardian*, 23 January.

210. Vidal, J. (2014), Norway has fallen in love with electric cars – but the affair is coming to an end. *The Guardian*, 29 January.

211. BBC News (2014), London crime falls 6% in a year say Metropolitan Police (22 April). Available at www.bbc.co.uk/news/uk-england-london-27117046 [accessed January 2015].

212. Changing London, 8 April 2014.

213. MOPAC (2013), Mayoral strategy on violence against women and girls: 2013–2017.

214. Caballero, M. (2004), Academic turns city into a social experiment. *Harvard University Gazette*. Available at http://news.harvard.edu/gazette/2004/03.11/01-mockus.html [accessed January 2015].

215. Moloney, A. (2014), Colombian women to party away as men face curfew night. *Reuters*, 8 October.

216. Metropolitan Police Service recorded crime figures and associated data, September 2014.

217. Stafford, M., Chandola, T., and Marmot, M. (2007), Association between fear of crime and mental health and physical functioning. *American Journal of Public Health* 97(11), 2076–81.

218. Changing London, 7 April 2014.

219. Mayor of London (2014), Strategy ambitions for London: gangs and serious youth violence. GLA.

220. Greater London Authority (2014), GLA health poll: topline results, March 2014.

221. Changing London, 25 February 2014.

222. Changing London, 18 February 2014.

223. See www.shiftdesign.org.uk/products/healthy-fast-food/ [accessed January 2015].

224. Changing London, 24 February 2014.

225. Burdett, R., and Taylor, M. (2011), Can cities be good for you? LSE Cities.

226. Changing London, 3 March 2014.

227. Changing London, 4 March 2014.

228. Changing London, 5 March 2014.

229. See www.cancerresearchuk.org/ [accessed January 2015].

230. Changing London, 19 February 2014.

231. Figures available from St John's Ambulance at www.sja.org.uk/sja/about-us/latest-news/hard-hitting-new-campaign.aspx [accessed January 2015].

232. Changing London, 26 February 2014.

233. Taylor, M. (2013), Speech by Matthew Taylor, Chief Executive, RSA, to Southampton Solent University (17 October).

234. Quoted in Sylvester, R., and Thomson, A. (2007), Will it be grumpy Gordon or father Brown? *Daily Telegraph*, 12 June.

235. Electoral Commission (2012), Greater London Authority elections 2012: report on the administration of the elections held on 3 May 2012.

236. Cathcart-Keays, A. (2014), From Klaus Wowereit to Hurricane Hazel: meet the longest-serving mayors. *The Guardian*, 26 August.

237. Lawson, N. (2012), Technology has created a flat earth where we can participate as equals. *The Guardian,* 4 March.

238. Changing London, 12 November 2013.

239. McKinsey (2013), How to make a city great: a review of the steps city leaders around the world take to transform their cities into great places to live and work.

240. Hanleybrown, F., Kania, J., and Kramer, M. (2012), Channeling change: making collective impact work. *Stanford Social Innovation Review,* 26 January.

241. Platt, S., ed. (1993), *Respectfully Quoted: A Dictionary of Quotations,* p. 194. Barnes & Noble.

242. *Encyclopaedia Britannica* (online), Andrés Manuel López Obrador [accessed January 2015].

243. Tizard, J. (2014), Constitutional debate must involve civil society. *New Start Magazine.* 22 September.

244. The quote is from Emily Dickinson's poem 'The Single Hound'. It reads: 'The Possible's slow fuse is lit. By the Imagination!'.

245. Stewart, N. (2012), DC citizens summit draws ideas, some criticism. *Washington Post,* 11 February.

246. Find out more at http://labplc.mx/ [accessed January 2015].

247. See, for example, www.korea4expats.com/article-pregnant-wo men-badge.html [accessed January 2015].

248. Find out more at www.nesta.org.uk/project/i-teams [accessed January 2015].

249. Johnson, B. (2014), 2020 vision: the greatest city on earth. GLA. Available at www.london.gov.uk/mayor-assembly/mayor/vision -2020 [accessed January 2015].

250. See www.sa2020.org/what-is-sa2020/ [accessed January 2015].

251. Edwards, T. (2014), Opposition to River Thames garden bridge plan grows. *BBC,* 16 October. Available at www.bbc.co.uk/news/uk -england-london-29627906 [accessed January 2015].

252. BBC (2014), London's River Thames garden bridge a 'vanity project' (9 January). Available at www.bbc.co.uk/news/uk-england-lon don-25671987 [accessed January 2015].

253. Blunden, M. (2013), Cyclists and pedestrians would share the first new Thames footbridge built in a decade. *Evening Standard,* 20 November. Available at www.standard.co.uk/news/transport/ cyclists-and-pedestrians-would-share-the-first-new-thames-foot bridge-built-in-a-decade-8951030.html [accessed January 2015].

254. Both figures from BBC news. Available at www.bbc.co.uk/news/uk-england-london-17961960 (for London) and www.bbc.co.uk/news/events/scotland-decides/results (for Scotland) [both accessed January 2015].

255. Ascherson, N. (2014), Scottish independence: the biggest surge of creative democratic energy the country has ever seen must not go to waste. *The Guardian*, 21 September.

256. Brooks, L. (2015), Scottish National Party 'mavericks' aim to tap into energy of yes campaign. *The Guardian*, 22 January.

257. Initiative and Referendum Institute at the University of Southern California. Available at www.iandrinstitute.org/Local%20I&R.htm [accessed January 2015].

258. Bryne, J., and Dizikes, C. (2014), Chicago voters want gun limits, no taxi fare hikes. *Chicago Tribune*, 19 March.

259. Willsher, K. (2014), Paris awaits result of referendum on how to spend €20m of city budget. *The Guardian*, 1 October.

260. Jones, S., Walker, P., and Wintour, P. (2013), Boris Johnson accused of dodging responsibility over cycling deaths. *The Guardian*, 14 November.

261. TfL (2013), The vision and direction for London's streets and roads: London Roads Task Force.

262. IBM Smarter Cities (2013), How to reinvent a city: mayor's lessons from the Smarter Cities Challenge.

263. Changing London, 13 January 2014.

264. Kidson, M., and Norris, E. (2014), Implementing the London Challenge. Joseph Rowntree Foundation/Institute for Government.

265. Changing London, 3 February 2014.

266. Changing London, 18 February 2014.

267. See www.london.gov.uk/mayor-assembly/mayor/mayoral-team [accessed January 2015].

268. Cruddas, J. (2014), Jon Cruddas's speech on power and belonging: full text. *New Statesman*. Available at www.newstatesman.com/politics/2014/05/jon-cruddass-speech-power-and-belonging-full-text [accessed January 2015].

269. Elbaek, U., and Lawson, N. (2014), The bridge: how the politics of the future will link the vertical to the horizontal. Compass.

270. Quoted in Luce, E. (2008), Politics and the policies of Barack Obama. *Financial Times*, 3 November.

271. Greater London Authority (2014), A wake up call for the mayor as rough sleeping rises (31 July).

272. Leadbeater, C. (2014), The London recipe: how systems and empathy make the city. Centre for London.

273. Changing London, 8 November 2013.

274. Quoted at www.biography.com/people/lyndon-b-johnson-9356 122 [accessed January 2015].

275. Changing London, 9 February 2015.

276. See www.prolificnorth.co.uk/2014/11/more-power-north-west -bbc-debate/.

277. Rogers, B. (2014), More powers for London will be good for the whole of Britain. *Evening Standard*, 17 November.

278. Smedley, T. (2012), Are urban environments best for an ageing population? *The Guardian*, 19 November.

279. World Health Organisation (2007), Global age friendly cities: a guide.

280. Changing London, 7 April 2014.

281. Changing London, 1 April 2014.

282. Changing London, 31 March 2014.

283. Changing London, 6 January 2015.

284. Changing London, 2 April 2014.

285. Treanor, J. (2014), Barclays AGM: shareholders large and small protest over pay and bonuses. *The Guardian*, 24 April.

286. Mulgan, G. (2014), Democracy makes itself at home online. Nesta.

287. Klose, C., and Haines, N. (2013), From little margins, big margins grow. *Inside Story*, 10 September.